JERUSALEM REVEALED

This volume contains articles adapted from

QADMONIOT

Quarterly for the Antiquities of Eretz-Israel and Bible Lands
Published in Hebrew by the Israel Exploration Society

Editor: Y. Yadin; *Associate Editor:* E. Stern; *Editorial Board:* M.
Broshi, A. Eitan, Y. Tsafrir, D. Ussishkin; *Hebrew Style:* R. Eshel;
Layout: E. Jacob; *Administrative Editor:* J. Aviram

English translation and abridgement by R. Grafman

JERUSALEM REVEALED

ARCHAEOLOGY IN THE HOLY CITY 1968—1974

EDITED BY YIGAEL YADIN

NEW HAVEN AND LONDON, YALE UNIVERSITY PRESS

AND THE ISRAEL EXPLORATION SOCIETY · 1976

PHOTO CREDITS
W. Braun; H. Burger; H. Cohen; S. Eldar; A. Glick; D. Harris; Israel Department of Antiquities
and Museums; Israel Museum; B. Lalor; A. Mazar; National Parks Authorithy; M. Pann;
Pantomap Israel Ltd.; Photo Emka, Jerusalem; Z. Radovan; R. Reich; J. S. Schweig; Y. Yadin.

Maps drawn by Carta, Jerusalem.

Originally published in Israel by the Israel Exploration Society in cooperation with
"Shikmona" Publishing Company.

Library of Congress catalog card number: 75-43338
International standard book number: 0-300-01965-3

Printed in Israel

079311

CONTENTS

LIST OF MAPS

COLOR PLATES

FOREWORD

Archaeological activity in Jerusalem between 1968 and 1974 revealed more of the city's past, within the Turkish walls, than did all the excavations in the same area in the last one hundred years. It is ironical that these excavations were indirectly brought about by the systematic destruction of the pre-1948 Jewish Quarter, including its numerous synagogues, during the period of Jordanian rule. Less than a year ago, UNESCO castigated Israel for these very excavations, holding that the character and history of Jerusalem were being altered. The present volume, however, is the best reply to that condemnation, exposing it — by way of contrast — as a clearly biased and politically motivated maneuver. Indeed, the government of Israel is to be commended for enabling the archaeological study of this ruinous area — eager as it is to further reconstruction and restoration without delay.

A key area in Jerusalem's history, the Jewish Quarter of the Old City is meticulously being excavated by Professor N. Avigad, shedding new light on the city's fortifications in the First Temple period and, for the first time, revealing the splendor of the Jewish secular architecture in the Second Temple period. At the same time, the excavations have revealed grim evidence of the thorough destruction wrought by the Romans upon the capital of the Second Jewish Commonwealth 1900 years ago.

The area of the Temple Mount remains out of bounds to excavational activities, and for obvious reasons the areas tangent to the Temple Mount have little been studied over the years, being hidden beneath the rubbish of centuries. All this has changed dramatically since the beginning of Professor B. Mazar's excavations in 1968 — the greatest archaeological enterprise Jerusalem has witnessed. His expedition, staffed by a most competent team, is working in a spirit of dedication and zeal befitting its historical mission. These excavations enable us to trace the history of the city step by step, stratum by stratum. The significant discoveries of Mazar and Avigad should in no way be allowed to blur the important work carried out in other parts of Jerusalem, by R. Amiran, D. Bahat, S. Ben-Arieh, M. Broshi, A. Eitan, and others.

This is the first of a series of English volumes, each of which is to be devoted to a specific topic, selected from among the material published in the Hebrew quarterly *Qadmoniot*. From its inception, *Qadmoniot* has given much space to reports and studies relating to Jerusalem. Indeed, the first issue, in 1968, was dedicated to the newly reunified city, and recently a second double issue has dealt with new discoveries there. The present volume contains all the material on Jerusalem published in *Qadmoniot* to date, translated and slightly abridged. The articles have been arranged so as to reveal the continuity of city life in Jerusalem, from Bible times to current plans for the future. The historical introductory articles enable even the layman to see the archaeological fieldwork in its proper perspective, and the specific studies discuss problems of antiquity (such as water supply and sanitation, and influences upon local arts and crafts) that are strikingly reminiscent of the contemporary city. The preservation of Jerusalem's unique heritage within a modern developing city is a matter of concern the world over, and the latter part of the volume gives the reader an inside view of the plans and problems involved.

For the reader's convenience, a general map showing most of the excavation sites in Jerusalem is given on page 23, while the tombs in the northern part of the city can be located on the map on page 63 (note also the map of the Jerusalem necropolis on page 131). The maps and tables of past excavations, on pages 131–35, are also most informative, going far beyond the scope of the material treated in the present volume. The general scheme of periods and dates, noted on page 131, can be referred to throughout the volume. The terms "First Temple" and "Second Temple" refer, respectively, to the Solomonic Temple, which met its destruction in 586 B.C.E., and the temple built by Zerubbabel in the 5th century B.C.E. Herod the Great dismantled Zerubbabel's structure, replacing it with a splended building of his own, which was destroyed in 70 C.E. In this volume (as is so often done), Herod's Temple has been included under the heading "Second Temple."

Much still remains to be done in the city. One of the greater challenges before us is the thorough excavation of the City of David. Though pioneer scholars were active here, it was only in recent years that significant light has been shed on the complex problems of this area of the city, during the major undertaking conducted by Dame Kathleen Kenyon which, indeed, prepared the ground for further research. Once this is accomplished, the full splendor of Jerusalem's five millennia will have been revealed, a "joy of all the earth" (Psalms 48:2).

YIGAEL YADIN

Jerusalem 1976

Jerusalem in the Biblical Period[*]

B. Mazar

A decisive development in the history of the Israelites in their own land came about in the period of the United Monarchy, raising Jerusalem to the status of a royal city, the metropolis and religious centre of the people. Indeed, the historiographical sources, the Prophets, the Psalms and other religious works preserved in the Bible and apocryphal literature, all devote much to the city's history, describing its strength and splendour — as well as the spiritual creativity — at its zenith, and its squalor in days of decline — foreseeing its renewed glory at the End of Days.

The name of the city, Jerusalem, seems to stem from its earliest days, for it finds mention already in the Egyptian "Execration Texts" of the 19th-18th centuries B.C.E., in a form probably to be read *Rushalimum*; in the el-Amarna Letters, of the 14th century B.C.E., it appears as *Urusalim*, and in the Sennacherib inscriptions (7th century B. C. E.), as *Ursalimmu*. The early Hebrew pronunciation was undoubtedly *Yerushalem*, as evidenced by the spelling in various inscriptions and by its form in the Septuagint. As for the meaning of the name, we can assume that it is a compound of the West-Semitic elements *yrw* and *šlm*, probably to be interpreted as "Foundation of (the god) Shalem" (cf. Yeruel, 2 Chronicles 20: 16 and Job 38 : 6). Shalem is known from a Ugaritic mythological text as one of the two "beautiful and gracious gods", Shahar and Shalim ("Dawn" and "Twilight", respectively). Salem, the shortened form of the name mentioned in Genesis 14 : 18 and Psalms 76 : 3, as well as in later sources, seems also to be quite early.

The city was known also as Jebus, an ethnic name denoting the population of the city and its "land" in the period of the Israelite Settlement down till its conquest by David. Arauna (*'wrnh, 'rwnh*), ap-

parently the last pre-Israelite ruler of the city, is thus called "Arauna the Jebusite". In the narrative of David's conquest, it is related that "the king and his men went to Jerusalem against the Jebusites, the inhabitants of the land...David took the stronghold of Zion, that is, the "City of David" (2 Samuel 6–7). The name "City of David" was given to the citadel of Zion by the king himself: "And David dwelt in the stronghold, and called it the City of David" (2 Samuel 5 : 9; 1 Chronicles 11 : 7).

The early name *Zion* specified the eastern hill of the city, with its northern summit ("Mount Zion)" known also as the "Temple Mount", the "mountain of the Lord", "mountain of the House of the Lord", where Solomon built the Temple and the royal palace; over the generations, the name Zion took on poetic connotations as an appellation for the entire city. Another name for the Temple Mount is "Mount Moriah" (2 Chronicles 3 : 1), the holy mountain in the "Land of Moriah" (Genesis 22 : 2), vestiges of some early, obscure tradition.

There are still other early names for Jerusalem, such as the "City of Judah" (2 Chronicles 25 : 28, as well as in the "Babylonian Chronicle"), denoting its nature as the capital of the kingdom of Judah, and "The City" (in the Lachish Letters).

The Pre-Davidic City

The archaeological finds and epigraphic and biblical evidence do not provide a well-founded basis for reconstructing the development and history of Jerusalem from its founding till its establishment as the royal city of the Israelite kingdom. Even so, archaeological research has been able to determine precisely where the city was located in earliest times — on the south-eastern spur below the Temple Mount. This small hill is protected by steep slopes on three sides: by the Kidron brook on the east, the Hinnom valley on the south, and the Tyropoeon

[*] Abridged from a comprehensive Hebrew article.

Air view of south-eastern hill of Jerusalem, looking north

valley on the west, which latter separates it from the western hill. Besides its conveniently defended location, the site possessed other advantages, suiting it as a focal settlement: It had an abundant spring, the Gihon, and it lay near the watershed and the principal highways — from Shechem to Hebron, and from the Coastal Plain to Jericho and the Jordan Valley — which crossed close by.

The many changes in the city's history, and the never-ceasing construction and destruction, have largely obliterated the remains of the early settlement here. Even so, we do have various data pointing to the continuity of settlement on this historical site, beginning in the Early Bronze Age. Already in the excavations of Parker (around 1910), pottery of the Early Bronze Age was discovered here (published by Vincent), namely painted ware of the Early Bronze Age I (early third millennium B.C.E.). An imported Cypriote bowl of the Middle Bronze Age I has also been found. Pottery of the Early and Middle Bronze Ages, as well as of the Late Bronze Age, has been found in the debris overlying bedrock in the various excavations carried out on the south-eastern spur and its slopes. Of greater importance is the discovery of the remains of a solid wall some 2.50 m thick, and of an adjacent tower built of rough boulders, on the eastern slope in the excavations undertaken by Dr. Kenyon. This fortification, it seems, was erected already in the Middle Bronze Age IIA (20th-19th centuries B.C.E.), and continued in use for a long time.

Also indicative of the early settlement here are the cemeteries of the Middle Bronze and the Late Bronze Ages on the western slopes of the Mount of Olives and in the Kidron brook, opposite the eastern hill. In one group, excavated on the site known as "Dominus Flevit" by the Franciscan Fathers, a very rich assemblage of pottery was discovered, along with a number of alabaster and faience vessels and Egyptian scarabs, mostly of the Middle Bronze Age IIC (16th century B.C.E.) and the Late Bronze Age I-IIA (15th-14th centuries B.C.E.). Especially instructive are the numerous vessels from the 14th century B.C.E., mostly from the first half of that century (the el-Amarna period), generally of the same types as found in a pit on the grounds of Government House, to the south of the city. These discoveries apparently indicate sporadic settlement outside the fortified city, and there is a surprisingly large number of imported pottery and other objects, especially those from Cyprus, the Aegean and Egypt.

Significant evidence on Jerusalem in the days of Egyptian rule in Canaan, in the first half of the 14th century B.C.E., is found in the el-Amarna Letters — diplomatic correspondence between the kings of various Canaanite cities and their overlords, Amen-hotep III and Amen-hotep IV (Ikhnaton). They include six letters sent by the ruler of Jerusalem to the

Foundation of Middle Bronze Age wall; right, segment of Israelite wall (*Kenyon excavations*)

Egyptian king, generally confirming the allegiance of the "Land of Jerusalem (*māt Urusalim*)". This ruler, ARAD-Ḫi-pa, "Servant of Ḫipa" (a Hurrian goddess), wrote in the *lingua franca* of that period, Akkadian, but the peculiarities of usage indicate that the language spoken in Jerusalem at this time was a West-Semitic dialect ("Canaanite"), closely related to the Hebrew of the Bible. He describes the situation in Canaan, requesting assistance in repelling Egypt's enemies — disloyal Canaanite rulers and their allies, the Habiru — and the rebelliousness of the locally-stationed Nubian troops, part of the Egyptian garrison in Canaan. Another interesting letter, sent by Shuwardata, the ruler of a city in the Shephelah, informs the Egyptian overlord of the great danger posed by the Habiru, especially after all his colleagues had abandoned him, only he and ARAD-Ḫi-pa remaining to fight them. These ties between local kings, as mentioned here and in other letters, fully reveal the importance of Jerusalem in the 14th century B.C.E. It seems that the land of Jerusalem extended in this period over a large area of the southern hill-country.

This picture may be of assistance in understanding the background of Joshua chapter 10, on the penetration of the tribes of Joseph (Ephraim and

3

Manasseh) to the west of the Jordan river, and their fanning out over the mountains of Benjamin and Ephraim. Jerusalem was still the most important kingdom in the southern part of the country. The Israelites came into contact with the Hivvite cities to the northwest and west of Jerusalem, the foremost of which was Gibeon, which apparently before the penetration of the Joseph tribes was subject to Adonizedek, the "Amorite" king of Jerusalem. The latter subsequently led an alliance of "Amorite" kings of the southern part of the country against Gibeon, and Joshua rushed to the aid of the city, defeating Adonizedek. Though this reduced Jerusalem's power, the city remained unconquered. In contrast to the Book of Joshua, Judges 1:8 tells of the sacking of Jerusalem by the tribe of Judah; if we assume that there were two waves of Israelite tribes in the 13th century B.C.E. (the "Rachel" or Joseph tribes and the "Leah" tribes, respectively), we can draw the following picture: Under the first wave, the king of Jerusalem was defeated but his city was not taken; while in the second wave the tribe of Judah succeeded in destroying the city. Unfortunately, the archaeological evidence is too meagre to substantiate or disprove this. We may note here that the Late Bronze Age vessels found in Jerusalem and its immediate vicinity are mostly of the 14th century B.C.E.

It is notable that the biblical sources treating the early population of Jerusalem and its neighbours to the south (for example Joshua chapter 10) use the term "Amorite", while towards the end of the period of Israelite settlement and at the beginning of the period of the Monarchy the term "Jebusite" appears in this context. It appears that Jerusalem was not Jebusite till the time of the Israelite Conquest, more specifically till the sacking of the city by the tribe of Judah. Some clue of the ethnic affiliation of the Jebusites may be hinted at in Ezekiel 16:3: "Thus says the Lord God to Jerusalem: Your origin and your birth are of the land of the Canaanites; your father was an Amorite, and your mother a Hittite." And we may note a well-known inhabitant of the city, Urijah "the Hittite." Equally of interest is the name of the owner of the site of the Temple Mount, who was probably the ruler of the city when conquered by David — Araunah (or *the* Araunah, as the Hebrew has it in one passage, cf. 2 Samuel 24:16) seems not to have been a personal name but rather the Hurrian word *ewrine*, "lord", which is found in Hittite (and as a personal name in Ugaritic), and refers to a ruler. Thus, the Jebusites are related to the Hittites and they came to control the "Land of Jerusalem", remaining a foreign enclave surrounded by the Israelites during the 12th–11th centuries B.C.E. (cf. Judges 19:10).

The City of David and the Temple Mount

The episode of the conquest of the Fortress of Zion and its becoming the City of David is described in 2 Samuel 5:6–9 as a daring deed on the part of the king, but in 1 Chronicles 11:4–7 it is ascribed to Joab, who thus gained his lofty position under David. We assume that David took Jerusalem early in his reign, prior to the events around the pool at Gibeon (2 Samuel 2:12–32) and the death of Abner (2 Samuel 3:20–27), at which time Joab was already the commander of the Judean army, and the foreign enclave between Judah and Benjamin had already been eliminated. The Jebusites were not wiped out, but rather continued to live "with the people of Benjamin in Jerusalem to this day" (Judges 1:21; cf. 1 Chronicles 11:8).

But David seems to have transferred his seat from Hebron to the new capital at Jerusalem some seven years after he had conquered the Fortress of Zion. In this period several events occurred which led to the strengthening of David's kingdom, and the new capital became the royal estate, forging a bond between the City of David and the Davidic dynasty. This relationship was a decisive factor in the history of the kingdom for generations to come.

There are few references in the Bible to David's building activities. His principal efforts — "And David built the city round about from the Millo inward" (2 Samuel 5:9: cf. 1 Chronicles 11:8) — should be ascribed to his earlier years in the city. The construction of the House of Cedars (apparently on the Millo) by craftsmen sent by Hiram, king of Tyre, can be regarded as having taken place later (2 Samuel 5:11). We may assume that David extended the fortified city on the north, towards the Temple Mount. This seems to have led to the breaching of the older city-wall on the north of the Fortress of Zion, till Solomon "closed up the breach of the city of David his father", strengthened the Millo (1 Kings 11:27), and began to erect his new

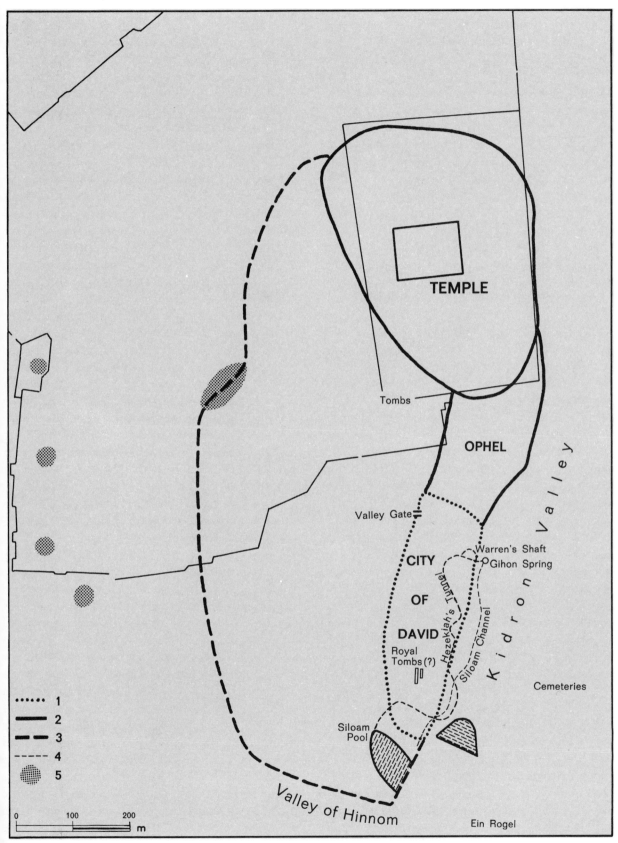

TEMPLE

Tombs

OPHEL

Valley Gate

Kidron Valley

CITY

OF

DAVID

Warren's Shaft
Gihon Spring

Hezekiah's Tunnel

Siloam Channel

Royal
Tombs (?)

Cemeteries

Siloam
Pool

Valley of Hinnom

Ein Rogel

...... 1
——— 2
— — — 3
– – – 4
⬤ 5

0   100   200
                m

Jerusalem in First Temple times. (1) Davidic wall; (2) Solomonic extension; (3) 8th–7th century extension; (4) subterranean water channels; (5) Israelite remains discovered on western hill acropolis, including the magnificent structures on the Temple Mount itself.

On the west of the spur there appears to have stood the "Valley Gate", in the vicinity of the later gate in the western wall of the City of David, discovered in Crowfoot's excavations. The "Millo" may well have been the terraces on the eastern slope of the south-eastern spur, forming supporting walls for the structures above. It seems to have been here that the more splendid of the buildings of the City of David were built, such as the "House of the Mighty Men" (Nehemiah 3 : 16) and David's "House of Cedars" and "David's Tower" (Song of Songs 4 : 4). Both man and nature had worked toward the obliteration of these structures, and even during the period of the Monarchy it was necessary to rebuild the Millo from time to time. Indeed, only retaining walls and a massive sub-structure at the middle of the slope, fragments of a Proto-Aeolic capital, ashlars and other meagre finds from the zenith of the Monarchy were discovered in the very limited excavations carried out here (by Dr. Kenyon).

When Jerusalem became the royal city of Israel, and the higher officials and permanent garrison were stationed there, David brought the Ark of the Covenant, symbolic of the unity of the tribes and of the covenant between the people and God. Thus, he established Jerusalem as the metropolis of the entire people and the cultic centre of the God of Israel. In the latter years of his reign, David built an altar on "Mount Zion", the Temple Mount; according to the tradition recorded in the Bible, David purchased the threshing floor of Aruna the Jebusite, upon God's command, for this purpose. It is clear that this site was held sacred even prior to David, for an elevated, exposed spot used as a threshing floor at the approaches to a city often served as the local cultic spot. The sanctity of Jerusalem, atop the Temple Mount, is inferred already in the Book of Genesis ("Mount Moriah"), though this is anachronistic. The tale of the connection between Abraham and Melchizedek, king of Salem and "priest of God Most High" — who blessed the Patriarch and assured him of victory over his adversaries, receiving a "tenth of everything" (Genesis 14 : 18–20) — is the outstanding example. Psalms 110 indicates the importance placed by tradition upon Melchizedek as an early ideal ruler, using his prestige to strengthen the claim on the city and the legitimacy of his successors there, the Davidic line. The story of the Sacrifice of Isaac (Genesis 22) is also revealing: The spot on one of the mountains in the land of Moriah, where Abraham built his altar, was the place called "the Lord provides", the site where David built his altar much later; thus, David is regarded as having rebuilt the altar of Abraham on this sacred spot.

The Royal Temple and the Royal Palace

The acropolis of Jerusalem, including the Temple and the royal palace, was apparently planned still during the coregency of David and Solomon, under the inspired guidance of Nathan the Prophet (2 Samuel 7). The actual construction, however, began only after the death of David, in the fourth year of Solomon's reign. The craftsmen, recruited from Tyre, laboured for some twenty years, and the buildings were built according to the typical plan of Neo-Hittite and Aramean royal cities in this period. This plan set off the "acropolis" — the royal precinct, with the military command and the civilian government, along with the priesthood — separate from the city proper. Solomon expressly built the Temple first, for it was not his intention merely to build a house for God and for the Ark of the Law, but further to establish the central Temple of Israel, under the patronage of the Davidic dynasty, to forge a perpetual bond between the royal line and the Temple, a bond which held all through the period of the First Temple.

Construction of the Temple lasted for seven years, and the palace complex — palace proper, the House of Pharaoh's Daughter, the throne-room, the Hall of Columns and the House of the "Forest of Lebanon" — was built immediately to the south, over a thirteen-year period. In both projects, Phoenician craftsmen were employed, and they left their imprint on the architecture, on the actual construction work and on the decoration and furnishings within. Solomon was also active in the City of David and its fortifications, and it has been suggested that the small segment of a casemate wall located near the top of the eastern slope of the northern part of the spur — discovered by Dr. Kenyon — should be ascribed to his reign. At this time the city already included within its walls not only the "acropolis" but also markets which were of considerable importance in international trade.

Proto-Aeolic capital found in Jerusalem, period of Judean monarchy (*Kenyon excavations*)

It may even well have been at this time that the city began its spread westward and northward, to areas outside the walls.

The City of Judah

From the time of the splitting of the Monarchy, following Solomon's death (ca. 930 B.C.E.), Jerusalem was the capital of the kingdom of Judah alone. Already at the end of Solomon's reign there arose factional differences between the royal family and the priesthood over division of authority between the secular and the religious powers. These differences recurred throughout the period of the Monarchy, with the varying strength of foreign influences, at first Phoenician, later Aramean, and finally Assyrian. Generally, this led to the strengthening of the purist faction, leading to religious reforms. All through this, the Temple continued to serve as a focal point of national-religious feelings, which first arose under David and Solomon.

The historiographical sources in the Bible relate much concerning the persistent efforts of the kings of Judah to fortify and glorify Jerusalem. Special importance seems to have been related to the establishment of the High Court in Jerusalem by Jehoshaphat (2 Chronicles 19). Of interest also are the descriptions of the repairs carried out in the Temple, such as those of Joash, as well as of the fortification work carried out in the city's defences. Uzziah and his coregent son, Joram, seem to have done much in the refortification of the city in the difficult days of Assyria's rise in the mid-8th century B.C.E. (2 Chronicles 26:9). Great attention was now given to the new citadel, which was built to the south of the Temple Mount, between the royal palace and the City of David.

A new phase in the history of Jerusalem began under Hezekiah, when the destruction of the kingdom of Israel, and its capital Samaria (722 B. C. E.), led to renewed ties between Judah and the remnant population of the northern kingdom. The new political and economic conditions which came about in the days of Sargon II of Assyria (722–705 B.C.E.) again raised Jerusalem to the status of a national-religious and economic centre for the entire nation. This enabled Hezekiah to achieve a strong position for his country between Assyria and Egypt, to extend the political borders of Judah in the Negev and in Philistia, "till Gaza", to take an important role in the trade with Egypt and Arabia, and to carry out religious reforms. However, the struggle of the Assyrian Empire for hegemony over the lands of the West, and its conflict with Egypt, brought Judah, too, into the maelstrom of war. Among the projects of Hezekiah in Jerusalem, on the eve of Sennacherib's campaign (701 B.C.E.), was to strengthen the Millo and the city-wall with its towers, and build a new wall (2 Chronicles 32:5), as well as the blocking of all sources of water outside the city; this also involved the diversion of the waters of the Gihon spring through the famous 'Siloam Tunnel" (see below, pp. 75 ff.).

Inscribed tomb plaque, Second Temple period, relating transfer
of bones of Uzziah, king of Judah

Another phase in the city's history began toward the end of the reign of Manasseh (968–642 B.C.E.), when that king was allowed to restore the autonomy of Judah, under Assyrian tutelage. Manasseh saw to the refortification of Jerusalem, the strengthening of its citadel and the building of a new outer wall (2 Chronicles 33 : 14). The city reached a new zenith, however, in the reign of Josiah (639–609 B.C.E.), when Judah threw off the Assyrian yoke, expanding its borders and influence, and undergoing an economic revival. During the reign of this king, the walled city of Jerusalem already included much of the area of the present-day Old City, including the Makhtesh (apparently in the Tyropoeon valley) and the Mishne (the western hill), undoubtedly the new residential and commercial centres of the city. The city's expansion to the west is clearly indicated by the various recent excavations on the western hill, and especially the discovery of a portion of a solid city-wall (see below, pp. 41 ff.). The height of Josiah's efforts was reached in his concentration of the cult in the Temple in Jerusalem, basing it on the Scroll of the Law — apparently the nucleus of the Book of Deuteronomy — discovered during repairs in the Temple (622 B.C.E.). With the restoration of the glory of the Davidic line,

the status of the Zadokite family of High Priests, which had served in the Temple in the days of Solomon, was restored; this dynasty of priests played an important role in Second Temple times as well, in both religious and political spheres.

After the destruction of Jerusalem and the Temple by the Babylonians (586 B.C.E.), the city continued to be the focal point of the national aspirations of the exiles and those who had remained in Eretz-Israel, and pilgrimages to the Temple Mount continued, not only from Judah but also from Samaria (Jeremiah 41 : 5). The decree of Cyrus, king of Persia (538 B.C.E.), gave expression to the reawakening of the Babylonian Exiles, and with the start of the Return, and the establishment of an altar, followed by the commencement of work on a new Temple, Jewish settlement was renewed in Jerusalem, and a major episode evolved in the history of the city.

The Jerusalem Necropolis

From the days of David on, it was custom to bury the kings in the City of David, at first in a royal tomb and subsequently in an adjoining cemetery. It may well be that the remains of tombs hewn into the rock, uncovered by Weill in the southern part of the south-eastern spur, represent the early royal cemetery of the Davidic dynasty. The later kings of Judah, and the members of the aristocratic families, were buried in a new necropolis (2 Chronicles 26 : 23), probably on the eastern slope of the western hill, near the western wall of the Temple Mount; and, from the time of Manasseh on, in the "Garden of Uzza", apparently in Siloam (see below, pp. 63 ff.).

The common populace of the city buried their dead mainly on the rocky slopes of the Mount of Olives, across the Kidron brook. We have noted above that this area was used for burial in much earlier times, and from the Israelite period on this became the principal cemetery for Jerusalemites throughout the generations. The tombs of the upper classes were centred around the Siloam village, and these cemeteries have played an important role in the consciousness of the Jewish people the world-over. Significantly, Nehemiah appealed to king Artaxerxes I to "send me to Judah, to the city of my fathers' sepulchres, that I may rebuild it" (Neh. 2 : 5).

Jerusalem of the Second Temple Period

M. Avi-Yonah

Toward the end of the Second Temple period, the walls of the city of Jerusalem, excluding the suburbs, reached an extent unrivalled till the 19th century. The fact that the city at that time was the spiritual centre of the Jewish people in widely scattered and wealthy communities was quite evident. Many of the regular inhabitants came from the four corners of the earth, and during the days of the three annual holidays of pilgrimage there was a tremendous influx of people into the city.

In the Second Temple period, the city was divided into two major parts for a considerable time. When Judas Maccabeus seized Jerusalem in 164 B.C.E. and rededicated the Temple, a part of the city around the "Akra" fortress remained in the hands of his enemies, together with a Syrian occupation force (see below, pp. 85ff.). This situation continued till 143 B.C.E., when Simeon the Hasmonean stormed the Akra, "and he entered it . . . with thanksgiving, and branches of palm trees, and with harps, and cymbals, and with viols, and hymns, and songs: because there was destroyed a great enemy out of Israel" (1 Maccabees 13 : 51). From that time on, Jewish control over Jerusalem was complete — till the destruction of the Temple in 70 C.E. From the latter date till recent years (except for a few years during the Bar Kokhba revolt and the Persian invasion), the city was controlled by non-Jewish rulers.

Thus, we may divide the period of the Second Temple into four sub-periods: the Persian period (the "Return from Exile"), the Hellenistic period, the Hasmonean period, and the Herodian period.

A long period of obscurity followed the active days of Ezra and Nehemiah. The city of then was small, spreading over the eastern hill from the Temple Mount southward. Dr. Kenyon's recent excavations here have revised the old theories that the wall discovered by Macalister and others on the "Ophel" hill here was the Jebusite city-wall. We now know that this was the wall rebuilt by Nehemiah, who himself described his work as a mere refurbishing of the city's defences, reducing the extent of the city. Nehemiah's city flourished within the framework of the Persian province of "Yehud", under control of the High Priests and Persian satraps. This situation continued for about a century, during which the city grew and its Jewish population increased, as did the Jewish population in the Babylonian diaspora; this was the incubation period for the great future of the city in its central, national-religious role.

The successors of Alexander the Great, the Ptolemies of Egypt (who controlled Jerusalem from 301 B.C.E.) and the Seleucids of Syria (who controlled it from 198 B.C.E. till its liberation by the Maccabees), removed Jerusalem from its isolation and made it part of the economic and cultural life of the Hellenistic world, placing it on a less spiritual plane. The economic activity of the Hellenistic period did not overlook the city, and its material growth enabled the High Priest, Simon the son of Onias (Simon "the Just") to carry out many projects: "In his life, [he] repaired the House [of the Lord], and fortified the Temple . . . and by him was built . . . the high fortress of the wall about the Temple: [and] in his days the cistern . . . was covered . . ." (Ecclesiasticus 50 : 1–3). The confrontation between the two elements, Jewish and Hellenic, soon came about; part of the city's population did not wish to continue the traditional, Eastern way of life, and they initiated the foundation of a new, "modern" town, outside the older, Oriental city. It was they who planned the expansion of the city to the western hill, abandoned since Nebuchadnezzar's siege. This new town was planned on the Hippodamian plan, with a regular network of intersecting streets. In the centre of this new quarter

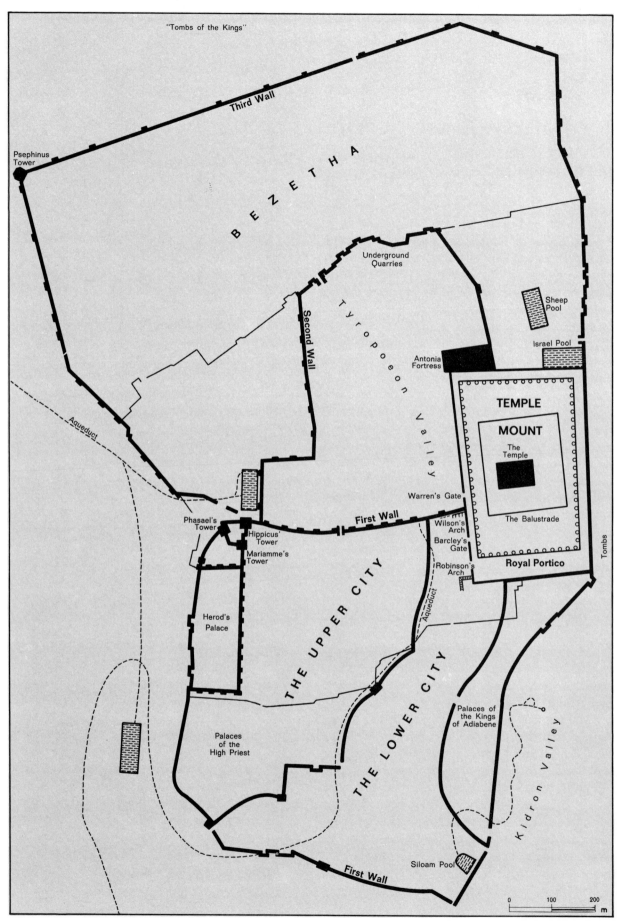

"Tombs of the Kings"

Third Wall

Psephinus
Tower

B E Z E T H A

Underground
Quarries

Sheep
Pool

Israel Pool

Second Wall

Antonia
Fortress

TEMPLE

MOUNT

The Temple

Tyropoeon Valley

Aqueduct

Warren's Gate

The Balustrade

Wilson's
Arch

Phasael's
Tower

First Wall

Barcley's
Gate

Hippicus'
Tower

Robinson's
Arch

Royal Portico

Tombs

Mariamme's
Tower

THE UPPER CITY

Herod's
Palace

Aqueduct

THE LOWER CITY

Palaces of
the Kings
of Adiabene

Kidron Valley

Palaces
of the
High Priest

Siloam Pool

First Wall

0   100   200
                    m

Jerusalem in Second Temple times

was the *agora*, or upper market, and at its eastern edge, opposite the Temple Mount across the Tyropoeon valley, the "Akra" fortress was erected, garrisoned by Greco-Syrian occupation troops.

During the entire Maccabean revolt, from 167 B.C.E. till the Jewish victory 15 years later, Jerusalem stood at the centre of events, though most of the battles took place away from the city. In keeping with their policy of utilizing the technological advances of the Greeks for the benefit of the Jewish state, the Hasmonean rulers preserved the "Upper City" as a part of the capital. After the Akra also fell into their hands (143 B.C.E.), and its fortifications were dismantled, Janneus built on its site a royal palace. This palace occupied the centre of the city and thus there were no special fortifications defending it. C.N. Johns, who excavated in the Jerusalem Citadel, has ascribed the early wall found by him to the Hasmonean period. In a logical extension of this, we can ascribe to them also the entire wall encompassing the rest of the western hill, stretches of which were exposed by Bliss in 1894–97, and recently by M. Broshi (see below, pp. 57 ff.). This city-wall joined up near the Siloam pool with the earlier wall of Israelite Jerusalem. It is clear that the Hasmoneans were interested in surrounding their capital with strong defences, and thus their fortification work finds mention in several places in the Books of Maccabees. The fact that Antiochus VII was forced to put the city to siege for an entire year further indicates that Jerusalem under the later Hasmoneans was a very strongly fortified city.

The course of the wall ascertained by Bliss and Johns ran from the corner of the city at the Citadel to the Temple Mount, on its northern line. It seems that there were two walls built within the city, on either side of the central Tyropoeon valley. The eastern of these two walls, on the western side of the "City of David", is well known. There seems to have been a second wall opposite, defending the lower eastern slope of the Upper City. The Hasmoneans joined the two parts of the city (the Temple Mount and the Upper City) by means of a bridge, a remnant of which today is called "Wilson's Arch". This is known mainly from the description by Josephus of Pompey's siege in 63 B.C.E.

In the Hasmonean period, till the death of Alexander Janneus, the land of which Jerusalem was capital expanded and flourished without limit. This undoubtedly influenced the character of the city, both materially and spiritually. The tombs in the Kidron valley and Jason's Tomb (see below, pp. 57 ff.) are almost the only substantial witnesses remaining from this cultural revival. Jason's Tomb, with the finds from within, is clear evidence of the continuation of early burial practices by the Hasmonean upper class; by this custom, all the bones of an entire family were collected in one burial chamber. Pharisee influence concerning the resurrection of the individual had not yet gained the upper hand. The grafitti in this tomb, depicting a naval battle, are indicative of the close connections between Hasmonean Jerusalem and the sea.

Some scholars ascribe to the Hasmoneans the construction, too, of the wall called by Josephus the "Second Wall". Today it represents one of the greatest mysteries in the topography of the city in Second Temple times. Josephus relates briefly that it ran from the "Gennath Gate" in the "First Wall" till the "Antonia Fortress", and that it encompassed the northern part of the city. It had relatively few towers (14), probably indicating its rather short course. But the line of this wall is still controversial. There are four major points for reconstructing it: Firstly, the site of the "Antonia Fortress" is quite certain, at the north-western corner of the Temple Mount. Secondly, the foundations of Damascus Gate comprise remains of the Herodian gate-towers. The placing of Damascus Gate along the line of the "Second Wall" necessitates the inclusion of the adjacent hillock on the east, as well. The inclusion of the Damascus Gate within the "Second Wall" is also necessitated by the identification of the "Third Wall", beyond. Thirdly, traces of quarrying running southwest from Damascus Gate may indicate the line of the wall here. Fourthly, Dr. Kenyon's and Dr. Ute Lux's excavations in the Muristan quarter and beneath the Church of the Redeemer have revealed that this area was outside the walled city in Second Temple times.

These four points would lead us to draw a line around the central valley and the markets within it. This line is not overly strong strategically, and its major motive may have been the protection of the commercial quarters from raiding and looting. Actually, the lay of the land on the north of Jerusalem is such that there is no proper line of defence

Joint of Phasael Tower and earlier city-wall, in courtyard of Citadel

between the central valley and the northern part of the Kidron valley, to the east; only much farther north was the "Third Wall" able to take advantage of the Kidron slope for defensive purposes.

Ascertaining the course of the "Second Wall" does not, however, solve the problem of its date. Of the two possibilities — Hasmonean or Herodian — the author would consider the latter as the more probable. Herod's fortifications near his palace and near Antonia indicate a need to strengthen the extremities of this wall. Nor does it seem to have existed at the time of Herod's siege and conquest of Jerusalem.

Jerusalem's independence came to an end shortly after the death of Alexander Janneus, the ruler under whom the Hasmonean state reached its peak. In 63 B.C.E., the Roman general Pompey stood within its gates. In 37 B.C.E. Herod, "King of the Jews" under Roman tutelage, took the city with foreign assistance and slaughtered many of its inhabitants. Under Herod, from 37 to 4 B.C.E., Jerusalem reached the height of its external splendour. Herod built a new administrative and defensive centre. This was accomplished by building a royal palace at the north-western corner of the Upper City, where he erected three towers to protect the palace as well as the weakest flank of the city. Today, only the base of the largest of the three towers is extant (see below p. 17). Johns' excavations within the Citadel here have proven that this Phasael tower was integrated into the earlier, Hasmonean city-wall by Herod's engineers.

Herod's palace, described by Josephus as having two main wings, surrounded by gardens, has not survived (except for its foundation platform; see below p. 53). Herod's placing the administrative centre of the city here held good until recent times, for the Tenth Roman Legion, after the destruction of 70 C.E., was garrisoned here as an occupation force, the Crusader kings had their palace here, and the Mamluk governors, succeeded by the Ottomans, held their courts here as well.

Herod's second major project was the renovation of the Temple Mount; here, too, this ruler was careful to ensure his authority, and he erected the Antonia Fortress on the saddle connecting the eastern hill with the northern ridge; actually, he rebuilt the earlier "Baris" fortress dating from Hasmonean times, thus gaining mastery over the outer Temple courts. The Temple Mount was expanded by Herod's engineers, doubling its area by means of huge supporting walls. This project involved changing the course of two valley-beds — the central, Tyropoeon valley, and a smaller valley on the north. The outer form given to the Temple Mount by Herod remains to this day. Dr. Kenyon, in her excavations, cleared part of the southeastern corner of the Temple Mount walls, further revealing the "seam" in the Eastern Wall there (see below, pp. 85 ff.); it is the present author's opinion that both sections of the wall here, on either side of the "seam", are Herodian, but belong to two phases of Herod's building project, the later, southern part being connected with the erection of the "Royal Portico" along the southern end of the mount; Robinson's Arch" belongs to this same phase.

Because of past difficulties, we know little more today about the Temple Mount than Warren did a century ago. The location of the actual Temple, the central problem, cannot yet be ascertained, though most scholars believe that the rock beneath the Dome of the Rock once formed part of the Temple, either part of the Holy-of-Holies or the base of the great altar. In the former view, the Temple stood stretching eastward, with the partition wall surrounding it touching upon the eastern portico; the other view regards this partition as having touched upon the western portico, which would seem more reasonable to us, for it is mentioned in the ancient sources that there was more open space on the east than on the west; since the entrance to the Temple was from the east, there was little need for stairs and gates on the west; and a wide space on the east would have provided room for viewing the fine façade of the Temple, which otherwise would have been largely obstructed (especially in the light of Herod's appreciation of fine architecture, evident throughout his works). Construction work on Herod's Temple continued till close to the time of its destruction, that is, till the days of the Roman Procurator Albinus. The general aspect of the city remained as Herod fixed it and in the 74 years between his death and its destruction we know of no major changes, though his grandson, Agrippa I, did undertake several projects of embellishment, initiating the construction of the "Third Wall" in the north.

This brief review has dealt principally with the material finds evidencing Jerusalem in the period of the Second Temple. The spiritual significance of the city in this period, however, obviously outweighed the material, and we may recall that it was then that the Bible began to crystallize in its final form, from the days of Ezra and Nehemiah on, with the Oral Law coming into existence later in the period, alongside various messianic trends, including the earliest Christianity as well as the Dead Sea Sect and its fascinating Scrolls.

The Architecture of Jerusalem in the Second Temple Period

N. Avigad

The period of monumental splendour in Jerusalem began with the spread of Hellenistic architecture into Eretz-Israel in the days of the Hasmoneans, and reached its zenith under the Herodian dynasty. Only meagre remnants of this architectural richness have survived, and it is familiar to us mainly from the literary sources, though the few extant remains are quite informative.

The Enclosure Walls
of the Temple Mount

Gazing down from the Mount of Olives towards the Temple Mount, one can observe the fine overall planning of the broad site. The present topography of the Temple Mount was made to conform to an overall plan for the Holy City. Only the outside, supporting walls of the Mount are preserved, but even these are most expressive of the might of Herod's project. The sanctity of the site to peoples other than the Jews has led to its being preserved even after the destruction of the Temple itself. The rectangular enclosure is broad and level; this "Haram esh-Sharif" ("Noble Enclosure") is identical in area with the Herodian Temple enclosure. The supporting walls measure as follows; west — 485 m; south — 280 m; east — 470 m; north — 315 m. The area enclosed thus measures some 142,00 sq.m. This expanse was formed by Herod's having built up the slopes and valleys flanking the earlier Temple Mount, and supporting the fill with huge retaining walls. Only in the north-western corner were his builders obliged to cut down the projecting rock surface to obtain the required level.

The basic concept here — that of a holy precinct or *temonos*, with the Temple at its centre — was common among various peoples in ancient times. The Temple Mount in Jerusalem, however, was much larger and much more splendid than other such precincts in the centres of the ancient world

The present level of the upper surface is at an average of 737.6 m above sea-level, and it can be assumed that the level of the Outer Court of the Temple varied little from this. The height of the supporting walls reaches some 30 m on the west, up to this level; in the south-eastern corner, this height is about 43 m, with a similar figure at the other southern corner.

Over the ages, much debris has accumulated against the walls of the Temple Mount and their upper parts have been destroyed and rebuilt several times. Thus, today only a few of the Herodian courses are generally exposed. Charles Warren, in the late 1860s, was forced by circumstances to dig shafts down to the lower levels, some distance away from the walls, which he then reached by means of horizontal tunnels. This painstaking and dangerous method enabled him to gain a picture of the lower courses of the walls and of the underlying bedrock. In spite of its obvious shortcomings, his work is still of utmost importance for research even today.

These walls, the classical example of the monumental character and fine quality of Herodian construction, are founded throughout directly upon bedrock. The ashlars have smooth margins surrounding a smooth, flat boss — all dressed with fine combing. The unexposed masonry was less refined but also of high quality. The ashlars, laid with extreme precision with no binder, are enormous in their dimensions: The average height is 1–1.20 m, and one course in the southern wall reaches 1.86 m (see below). The ashlars vary in length from one metre to three and more; one outstanding stone at the south-western corner is almost 12 m long! The heaviest stones weigh about 100 tons. The walls are somewhat battered, successive courses being slightly offset.

The
Western
Wall

The Western Wall. The southern half of this wall has been investigated, with emphasis on three main features here: "Robinson's Arch", "Wilson's Arch", and "Barclay's Gate". In the centre of this portion is the so-called "Wailing Wall"; after the 1967 war, some 57 m here were exposed, from "Barclay's Gate" up to the Mekhkeme building. The seven lowermost exposed courses here are Herodian; above are Roman, Byzantine and more recent courses. There are 19 further Herodian courses yet buried, rising 21 m from the bedrock. At the southern corner, there are six courses with crude bosses; they had obviously never been exposed and are below the level of the marble pavement discovered already by Warren. There are 16 fine Herodian courses extant above the cruder masonry (see below, pp. 25-27).

It should be noted that all these courses are below the level of the Court of the Temple Mount. Only at the northern end of the Western Wall, where the bedrock is quite high, is any Herodian masonry higher than the floor-level of the Mount; these ashlars resemble the masonry of the pilasters of the Herodian exterior of the Haram el-Khalil in Hebron.

Some 11.50 m from the southern corner, three courses jut out from the Western Wall for a length of 15.50 m — the skewback of "Robinson's Arch", the remains of a monumental staircase leading from the Temple Mount down to the Tyropoeon valley (see below, pp. 25-27).

Some 180 m north of the corner is a vaulted, subterranean structure today called "Wilson's Arch". It is 13.40 m wide and thought to be the first arch of a bridge crossing the Tyropoeon valley to the Upper City on the west. Some 82 m north of the corner, there is an early opening in the wall, known as "Barclay's Gate", hidden within more recent structures. Its huge lintel is 7.50 m long and 2.08 m high. The opening is about 8.76 m high, but the threshold is missing (it probably had been at the 722.7 m level). This gate seems to have had a staircase leading up to it and through it to the Temple Court.

The Southern Wall. The western corner of this wall lies up the eastern slope of the western hill, with the original bed of the Tyropoeon valley some 30 m to the east (697.5 m level). The wall thus crosses the valley bed and is presently 26 m high at this corner. The bedrock rises to the east where, at the "Double Gate", it is at about the 726 m level, descending again to the Kidron valley, being at the 684 m level at the south-eastern corner of the Temple Mount. This is the most impressive corner of the walls, with 35 Herodian courses reaching some 48 m high.

There is one course in this wall, the 28th from the bottom, which is unusually large, 186 m high; it is known today as the "master-course" and runs from the eastern corner to the "Double Gate", for some 183 m. It appears to have formed a sort of dado along the street running before the gates here (see below, pp. 27-28).

There are three gates in the Southern Wall, all presently blocked. On the east is the "Single Gate", apparently of Crusader date. The other two gates, the "Double Gate" and the "Triple Gate", are Herodian and represent the "Huldah Gates" mentioned in the Mishna. The thresholds of these two gates are about 12 m below the level of the Court above; that is, they are two courses higher than the probable threshold of "Barclay's Gate". Tunnels lead up from either gate to the Court of the Temple Mount.

The "Double Gate" is about 100 m from the western corner and is partly hidden by later structures. It is about 12.80 m wide, with a thick pier in the centre, dividing it into two openings. Within is a square hall with a column at the centre, supporting arches upon which four low domes rest, with pendentives in the corners; one of the domes still bears stucco ornamentation, in an Eastern Hellenistic style.

The present form of the "Triple Gate", with three openings, is late. Originally it, too, was probably a double gate; one part of its western jamb is Herodian.

A street running before the gates was reached by means of several broad monumental staircases (see below, pp. 26-30).

The Eastern Wall. The great accumulations of debris have hindered investigation of this wall. Near the southern corner, the masonry resembles that of the Southern and Western Walls. About 31 m from the southern corner there is a vertical "seam" apparently for the entire height of the wall; to its north, the masonry has only crude bosses. It is believed that this indicates two different periods of construction (but see above and below, pp. 13, and 85–86).

Some 310 m from the southern corner there is a gate structure, known today as the "Golden Gate" or the "Gate of Mercy", the only extant gate in the Eastern Wall of the Temple Mount. It is now blocked and its threshold is on a level some 7 m below that of the surface of the Temple Mount. The present gate is probably from the late Byzantine period, though some scholars hold that it was built over an older gate. At this spot the base of the wall is some 43 m below the surface of the Temple Mount, mostly hidden below the outside ground-level.

The northern portion of the Eastern Wall, 26 m long, juts out some two metres from the line of the wall. At this corner, 5–11 Herodian courses are preserved, the second spot in which Herodian courses are found above the level of the surface of the Temple Mount. The bedrock is located here some 20 m below the surface.

The Northern Wall of the Temple Mount has been little studied, its situation being unfavourable for investigation.

The Phasael Tower

An important remnant of one of Herod's structures is located in the Jerusalem Citadel, near Jaffa Gate. Here, in the Upper City, stood Herod's palace, protected on the north by three huge towers: Hippicus, Phasael and Mariamne. The Phasael tower is most often identified with the lower portion of a square, solid structure commonly called "David's Tower", in the north-east of the Citadel. This identification is based on the dimensions given by Josephus in his description of the base of the Phasael tower, which closely correspond with the measurements of this structure (see below, pp. 52 ff.). The upper part of "David's Tower" is a later addition.

The height of the ancient base is 19.85 m, built in two parts, each one of eight courses. The upper part is 17.12 m wide and 21.40 m long, and the lower part is slightly larger (18.30 × 22.60 m). This solid structure is outstanding in the quality of its typically Herodian masonry.

Josephus relates that the towers here were built within "the ancient wall", and indeed, during excavations in the Citadel (see below, pp. 52 ff.), it was ascertained that the Phasael tower was set into

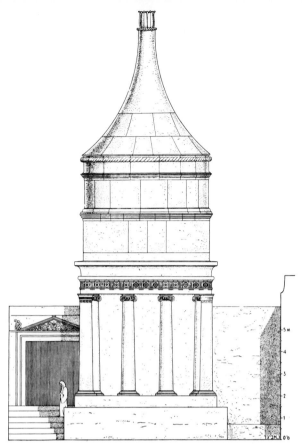

"Absalom's Tomb", with façade of "Jehoshaphat's Tomb" on left

part of the city-wall, some of which is from the Hasmonean period.

The Necropolis

Jerusalem of the period of the Second Temple possessed a necropolis which encompassed the city on every side. So far, hundreds of tombs have been found hewn into the rock in the form of subterranean chambers. Generally, the only trace of them visible on the surface is a small opening; occasionally, however, they possess façades with architectural ornamentation carved into the rock, and at times entire structures were carved out of the rock or constructed as memorial monuments.

Though specific concepts were dominant in the tomb architecture, generally there was no standardization and each tomb possesses a character of its own. The most common architectural styles were the Doric and Ionic (capitals and friezes); the Corinthian is lacking altogether and the Egyptian is represented only by the pyramid form and the concave cornice. Very typical of the architecture of the Jewish tombs of this period is a composite style, a mixture of elements of the several styles. Generally, this style is influenced by the Eastern

17

Hellenistic architecture, but it is peculiar to Jewish art.

In the portion of the Kidron brook opposite the Temple Mount, the slope of the Mount of Olives terminates in a rock-scarp into which several monumental tombs have been carved. From south to north, these are the "Tomb of Zachariah", the Tomb of the Bene Hezir, the "Tomb of Absalom" and the "Tomb of Jehosaphat". Except for the Bene Hezir Tomb, the names are mere folk attributions and lack all historical basis.

Chronologically, the Tomb of the Bene Hezir is earlier than its neighbours, and it is apparently to be ascribed to the Hasmonean period, at the start of the first century B.C.E. It comprises a series of subterranean burial chambers and has a façade hewn into the rock-scarp, some 45 m above the valley floor. In the opening of the porch stand two Doric columns between pilasters ("distyle in antis"), topped by a Doric frieze. We may mention that the purely Doric style of this façade is in contrast to the more typical composite style of most of the tomb monuments in the Jerusalem necropolis. On the architrave over the columns, there is an incised Hebrew inscription, reading: "This is the tomb and monument of Eleazar, Hania, Joezer, Judah, Simeon (and) Johanan, sons of Joseph son of Obed; Joseph and Eleazar, sons of Hania, priests of the Bene Hezir." The "monument" mentioned here is probably at the continuation of the façade to the north, where a wall with a simulated entrance is carved; this latter had most probably been capped by a small pyramid, in ancient times a structure symbolic of tombs.

Immediately to the south is the so-called "Tomb of Zachariah". This tomb is hewn out of the rock and is free-standing, surrounded by high walls of sheer rock; it is made up of two major parts; the actual building, in the form of a cube measuring 5 × 5.50 × 7.50 m, with a pyramid atop, 4.70 m high. All four of its sides are ornamented with engaged columns with Ionic capitals and corner pillars bearing an Egyptian cornice. The lower part of this monument was, until a decade ago, hidden beneath much later Jewish graves, located here because of the sanctity attached to the spot. After these latter had been cleared away, the lower part of the façade was revealed, with an opening to a small, irregular chamber hewn into the rock below.

A more variegated composite style is to be seen in the third monument of this group, the so-called "Tomb of Absalom". This monument is most impressive in its complete and special form, which has no exact parallel in contemporaneous architecture. It is free-standing and rises some 20 m. Its two principal parts are a lower cube and an upper drum and cone. Most of the square structure is carved out of the bedrock, to a height of 8 m; it terminates in a course of large ashlars and is ornamented on all four sides with engaged Ionic columns, with a Doric frieze of triglyphs and metopes (containing rosettes) and an Egyptian cornice above. Within the square structure is a burial chamber, with an entrance on the south, some 8 m above ground-level.

The round structure is built entirely of ashlars. It comprises a drum and a concave conical roof, crowned by a stone carved in the form of a multi-petalled flower. The round structure is to be interpreted as the "monument", denoting the tomb found within the square structure below. This architectural concept has close parallels in the rock-hewn tombs at Petra and other sites. Hellenistic and Roman monuments of similar form also have a square base and a structure in the form of a round temple (*tholos*) above, with columns and a conical roof. In the "tholos" of "Absalom's Tomb", only the columns are missing, possibly to avoid resembling a pagan temple. On the basis of style, this tomb should probably be ascribed to the start of the first century C.E.

We can assume that, besides its being a tomb and a monument at one and the same time, "Absalom's Tomb" also served as the monument for the catacomb of the adjacent "Tomb of Jehosaphat". The two tombs were hewn contemporaneously. The façade of the "Tomb of Jehosaphat" possesses a large, ornamented entrance (gable with carved acanthus leaves, tendrils and fruit) in the decorative style of the Jewish art of the end of the Second Temple period.

The custom of setting up monuments for the spirit of the deceased is further witnessed in the three small pyramids which had stood atop the Tomb of Queen Helene, as described by Josephus (*Antiquities* XX, 4, 3). This tomb, popularly known as the "Tomb of the Kings (of Judah)", is located north of the Old City; it is the largest and one of the most impressive tombs in Jerusalem. Queen Helene of Adiabene (in northern Mesopotamia), who had

Façade of "Tomb of the Kings" (restoration)

been converted to Judaism, was buried in Jerusalem sometime after 50 C.E. A broad staircase (9 m wide and some 30 m long) descends to a sunken courtyard hewn into the rock (26 × 27 m). The façade and opening to the corridor of the tomb-cave, partly destroyed, was distyle *in antis*. Its outstanding ornamentation had a Doric frieze with a bunch of grapes flanked by wreaths and acanthus leaves at its centre; a wreath band with fruit and pine-cones ornamented the architrave in a decorative band. The opening to the tomb-cave proper was closed by a "rolling stone". The catacomb comprises eight chambers, with niches and arcosolia. The tomb was found to contain several ornamented sarcophagi; one bore the name of "Queen Saddan".

Another apparently royal tomb is the "Tomb of the Family of Herod", located to the west of the Old City, adjacent to the King David Hotel. This is generally identified with the monument mentioned by Josephus in his description of the Roman siege dyke in this region (*War* V, 3, 2, 108; XII, 2, 507). Its plan differs from that of the other tombs:

Four chambers surround a smaller central one; the walls of the chambers are faced with ashlars, an uncommon practice in Jerusalem (but see below, pp. 66 f.). The entrance was closed by a "rolling stone", unusually large. Within the chambers were several sarcophagi, bearing floral ornamentation. Before the entrance there are traces of what was apparently a monument.

The second monumental tomb discovered to the west of the Old City is "Jason's Tomb", comprising two courts, a porch and two burial chambers. It has a single Doric column in the façade, *in antis*, instead of the usual two columns. Above the tomb was a pyramid, some stones of which were discovered. On the walls of the porch are several laments, written in Aramaic and Greek, mentioning the name Jason, together with grafitti of ships at sea. On the basis of the finds from within, the tomb is from the first century B.C.E., in the time of the Hasmoneans.

One of the few tombs which can be connected with a personage known to us from literary sources

Façade of Umm el-'Amed tomb (restoration)

is that of Nicanor, on the grounds of the Hebrew University on Mount Scopus. It contained several ossuaries, one of them bearing an inscription in Greek indicating that it contained the bones of the sons of Nicanor of Alexandria (who had donated the bronze doors of the Temple), followed by the names Nicanor and Alexa, in Hebrew characters. This catacomb is one of the most intricate in Jerusalem, and includes a large courtyard, a corridor and four branches of burial chambers, spreading out over several "storeys". The façade was distyle *in antis*.

Near the Tomb of Nicanor, the burial-vault of a Nazirite family has also been discovered (see below, pp. 66 ff.).

A large group of rock-hewn tombs is located to the north of the Old City, the most famous being the "Tombs of the Sanhedrin". The main entrance of this tomb is crowned by a gable with acroteria — the most pleasing of the gables on tomb-façades in Jerusalem. Stylized acanthus leaves fill the entire triangle, with pomegranates and other fruit scattered among them. The motif, style and execution are typical of Jewish decorative art. This catacomb uniquely has two rows of niches hewn in the walls of its chambers, one above the other, providing for some 70 burial places within the one tomb (and thus the popular ascription to the Sanhedrin).

Of two other tombs with notable façades, located in the same general region, one has a gable and acroteria over the entrance, with vine tendrils and bunches of grapes in a free composition; the other is distyle *in antis*. Another tomb is unique in its having a sarcophagus bearing a rosette pattern, hewn out of and still attached to the bedrock.

A tomb located north of the northern group of tombs, across the Kidron brook, is the tomb known as the "Cave of Umm el-'Amed". This comprises two burial chambers and a porch; the façade is mostly destroyed, but it had been a most splendid tomb externally, with a façade and walls of the porch hewn into the rock and dressed as if built of ashlars in the Herodian style. The opening was distyle *in antis*. On the upper part of the façade are traces of an unusual combination of styles: a Doric frieze with rosettes and, above, a row of dentils (a definite Ionic feature) with guttae (a typical Doric element) pendent below. The Umm el-'Amed tomb, more than any other, enables us to assume that the tomb-architecture of Jerusalem was not an isolated style, but rather derived from the general architecture of the period. And it is very probable that this is highly indicative of the style and form of building in Jerusalem in this period in general, though essentially no true building remains have survived to confirm this.

Excavations in Jerusalem—Review and Evaluation

M. Avi-Yonah

In the second half of the 19th century, when conditions in Palestine first permitted archaeological excavations like those being carried out in Egypt and Mesopotamia, scholars unhesitatingly regarded Jerusalem as the primary site for investigation. The first excavators, De Saulcy and Warren, initiated their projects here — De Saulcy not very successfully in the "Tombs of the Kings", and Warren by an extensive exploration around the walls of the Temple Mount (1867–69). Warren's excavations still today arouse the admiration of archaeologists, both for his amazing persistence and for his accuracy, borne out in general by later work. Later excavators came to realize that Jerusalem was undoubtedly the most difficult site in the country to excavate. In this city, the destroyers — and the builders even more so — have wreaked a havoc which can be unravelled only by supreme effort and most exacting labour. Moreover, the objects found are relatively meagre, especially when seen in the light of the splendid treasures being found in Egypt and Mesopotamia. A further reason for disappointment was the fact that the finds were mostly from the post-biblical period, and at the end of the 19th century the interest of the investigators was especially directed toward the Bible. Thus, it is not surprising that, after the initial probings, there was an extended hiatus in scientific excavation in Jerusalem. Several sites were, however, cleared — especially churches, and mainly with the intent of erecting new buildings on their sites. Under the British Mandate, archaeological work concentrated on the hill of the "City of David" — the archaeologists' "Ophel hill" — that is, in an area outside the present-day walls of the Old City. Weill began clearing the southern extremity of the hill (1913–14; 1923–24). Macalister's excavations (1923–25) and those of Crowfoot (1927–29) on the "Ophel hill" did not add much to our knowledge beside the discovery of the western gate of the "City of David" (by Crowfoot), but this feature, too, is difficult to date. Besides these, two excavations were carried out in the north and in the west of the Old City: In 1925–27, L.A. Mayer and E. L. Sukenik cleared the remains of a wall on the north of the city, identifying them with Josephus' "Third Wall" (for which see below, pp. 60 ff.). C.N. Johns excavated on behalf of the Mandatory Department of Antiquities in the courtyard of the Citadel (1935–40), where he uncovered part of the Hasmonean city-wall — actually the north-western corner of the "First Wall". Johns was able to demonstrate that the Phasael Tower, built by Herod, was only later worked into this wall.

The Second World War, the following period of unrest, and the War of Independence brought a halt to archaeological work in Jerusalem for more than a decade. Only late in the period of Jordanian control was work again initiated — by Dr. Kathleen M. Kenyon and her expedition staff (1961–67), mainly in the "City of David". Several very limited trial soundings were made within the Old City, on "Mount Zion", near Damascus Gate and near the "Third Wall". At the same time, limited work was being carried out at several Christian sites: in the Holy Sepulchre, in the area of "Antonia Fortress" (Convent of the Soeurs de Sion) and near the Bethesda Pools. These excavations served mainly to raise doubts concerning several accepted generalities in the topography of Jerusalem in the Second Temple period (see below, pp. 87 ff.).

The reunifying of Jerusalem in 1967 enabled widespread excavation activity, much of which is described elsewhere in this volume. The present review outlines the innovations and changes stemming from the excavations and publications of this past half-decade (except those dealt with specifically below). The latest excavations have provided more positive data than all the previous years combined.

Concerning the problems of Jerusalem in the period of the First Temple and earlier: By ascertaining that the Jebusite city-wall (and the wall of the subsequent "City of David") ran along the middle of the eastern slope of the eastern hill, Dr. Kenyon has solved one of the most difficult problems in the topography of ancient Jerusalem. The earlier belief that the eastern wall of the "City of David" ran at the top of the slope left the upper outlet of Warren's shaft outside the supposed line of the wall. According to Dr. Kenyon's proposal, both the entrance to the shaft and the tunnel were within the walled city. This in turn indicates that the Jebusite city and the "City of David" spread over a much larger area than previously considered. She was not able, however, to connect in a reasonable manner the line of the city-walls with the Siloam Pool of Hezekiah.

The problem of the northern end of the "City of David", and that of the expansion to the western hill (Josephus' "Upper City"; today's Jewish and Armenian Quarters, together with "Mount Zion", outside the modern walls) have not entirely been solved. The excavations of Mazar, Avigad, Amiran and Eitan, and Broshi have fixed two basic facts: There *was* an Israelite settlement on the western hill, at first unwalled and later fortified at least in part by a stout wall—from the 8th century B.C.E. on. The early existence of the "Mishne" quarter has been proven by pottery and building remains which have been discovered directly on bedrock, within a layer of reddish earth (see below, pp. 41 ff.). It was also ascertained that the central valley between the eastern and western hills was outside the city until the 8th century B.C.E.; this is evidenced by tombs hewn within the valley in the 9th-8th centuries B.C.E. The continuation of the wall discovered by Avigad is still unclear, either on the north or on the south. We may assume, however, that on the south this wall joined up with the wall of the "City of David", encompassing the Siloam Pool. This serves to solve the problem of why Hezekiah brought the waters of the Gihon spring "within the city", to a reservoir once thought not to have had a defensive wall.

In the days of Nehemiah, the city seems to have shrunk again, being limited to the eastern hill. The wall and towers at the top of the slope, previously ascribed to First Temple times, are now to be considered Hasmonean, for they overlie ruins of houses from the period of the kingdom of Judah.

One very important point has been settled in the excavations near the Western Wall of the Temple Mount: In contrast to previous theories, it was ascertained that "Robinson's Arch" was not a bridge between the Temple Mount and the Upper City, but merely a span supporting stairs leading down from the Mount (see below, pp. 25 ff.). The situation south of the Temple Mount is also clearer, revealing a quite detailed picture of the approaches to the Huldah Gates, the main entrance to the Temple precincts for the pilgrims.

It is now clear that there was only one bridge leading across the Tyropoeon valley—that of "Wilson's Arch", north of the Western Wall plaza. Here, debris have been cleared and the site prepared for tourism by the Ministry for Religious Affairs.

In the area of the Upper City, in contrast, considerable new data have been obtained, greatly clarifying the picture. Work in the Armenian Garden has confirmed that the "First Wall" on the western flank indeed lay beneath the present city-wall there. The excavations in the north-eastern part of the Jewish Quarter enable us to locate the Hasmonean palace and possibly also the site of the Seleucid Akra (but see below, pp. 85 f.). It would seem that Antiochus IV prepared huge columns (see below, p. 50) for a temple (of the Olympian Zeus?) in the Hellenistic city he intended to found.

As for the Herodian period, in the recent excavations in the courtyard of the Citadel and in the Armenian Garden, identical remains were found of the foundation platform on which Herod's palace had been built. Of the palace itself nothing remains, but we can certainly determine that this building stretched from the Citadel to around the south-western corner of the Old City. In Tushingham's excavations (within the framework of Dr. Kenyon's expedition), further remains of this platform were encountered, though the excavators did not appreciate the significance of their find (see below, pp. 55 f.).

The houses of the Herodian and subsequent periods in the area of the Upper City bring the late Second Temple city to life—from the upper class house covered over already in Herod's day by a street ascending opposite "Robinson's Arch", to the burnt Kathros family house (see below, p. 45). To

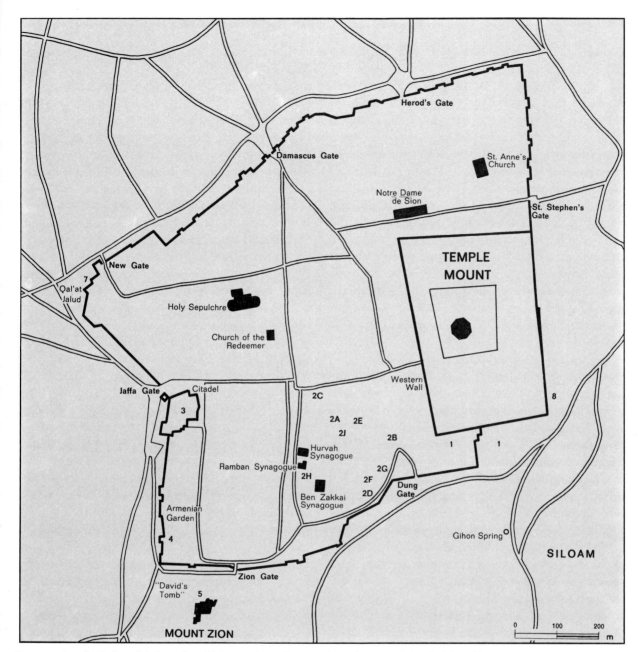

Recent archaeological work in Jerusalem. (1) Excavations adjacent to Temple Mount (Mazar); (2) Jewish Quarter excavations (Avigad); (3) Citadel excavations (Amiran & Eitan); (4–5) Mount Zion excavations (Bahat & Broshi; Broshi); (6) Third Wall examination (Ben-Arieh); (7) Tancred's Tower examination (Bahat & Ben-Ari); (8) Seam in eastern Temple Mount wall (see pp. 16 and 85–86)

these we may add the contemporaneous house uncovered by M. Broshi in the area of the Armenian cemetery on "Mount Zion", notable for its frescoes. These latter include depictions of birds in the style of Pompeii — a so-far unique find for this country (see below, pp. 49, 58 , and Pl. III). Evidence of adherence to the injunction against depicting animal forms is found in the mosaic pavements found in other houses, with purely geometric patterns (see Pl. II). The Herodian houses in the southern section of the Jewish Quarter generally were built directly over the Israelite strata. Besides these "temporal" dwellings, we should note the necropolis of Jerusalem in the Second Temple period — the tombs on the Mount of Olives, the tomb of "Simon the Temple Builder" (see below, pp. 71 f.) and of "Yohanan" who had been crucified, on Giv'at Hamivtar, and the tomb of the Nazirite on Mount Scopus (see below, pp. 66 f.) — all giving new dimension to the cemeteries surrounding the city, alongside the long-known

23

"Tombs of the Kings", Herod's Family Tomb, the Tomb of Nicanor and others.

North of the Temple Mount, our picture has been clarified by the excavations within the Convent of the Soeurs de Sion and in the area of the Bethesda Pools. In the former, it was ascertained that the pavement — previously identified with the *lithostrotos* (mentioned in John 19 : 13) and with the court of the Antonia Fortress — was in fact contemporaneous with the "Ecce Homo" Arch, erected in the 2nd century C.E. as part of Aelia Capitolina. In the opinion of P. Benoit (see below, pp. 87 ff.), there is no archaeological basis for the accepted reconstructions of the Antonia Fortress as a very extensive structure with four massive corner towers; the fortress was limited, apparently, to the area between the Temple Mount and the "Via Dolorosa", or even less than this.

The second discovery concerns the Bethesda Pool, also mentioned in John (5: 2–4). In the excavations since 1956, it was found that the two pools there were Hasmonean, and that they went out of use with the building of "Birket Israin", along the "Northern Wall" of the Temple Mount. The miracles performed at this spot by Jesus, according to Christian tradition, are now ascribed to a cave east of the above pools. The waters of a nearby brook were gathered in this cave and, because of their reddish colour, were held to have healing properties.

The problem of the "Second Wall" of Jerusalem in the days of the Second Temple — so prominent a subject in the topographical controversy — is still far from solution. Dr. Kenyon made a trial sounding in an open space near the Lutheran Church of the Redeemer, where she found layers of rubble down to bedrock. The results have been confirmed by excavations of the German Archaeological Institute in Jerusalem, directed by Ute Lux, beneath the foundations of the very church; it was ascertained that the wall beneath the church, ascribed since its discovery in the 1800s to the "Second Wall", is actually from the days of Agrippa I, at earliest. Since the "Second Wall" was located in its entirety within the present-day Old City walls (reaching at most to the Damascus Gate), it is impossible to ascertain its course at present.

The controversy surrounding the course of the "Third Wall", too, is still alive. Hennessy, who excavated in front of Damascus Gate, ascribed the triple gate there, with its flanking towers, to the "Third Wall". His conclusions are based on an examination in a very limited area at the eastern gate and tower, and disregard Hamilton's results from 1937, near the western gate there. Neither Hennessy nor Dr. Kenyon could explain satisfactorily the massive foundations of a wall discovered by Mayer and Sukenik far to the north. In the last few years, another attempt was made to settle this controversy, just outside the north-western corner of the Old City walls, but only a wall and fosse of the Crusader period were found (see below, pp. 109 f.), the medieval builders having thoroughly destroyed all earlier structures there. Excavations currently being conducted on the line of the Mayer-Sukenik wall seem to be leading to a solution of this difficult controversy (see below pp. 60 ff.).

The excavations adjacent to the Temple Mount and in the Jewish Quarter have greatly supplemented our knowledge of the development of the city following the destruction of 70 C.E. Thus, the camp of the Tenth Roman Legion, stationed here from 70 C.E. to the third century C.E., is now considered to have been much larger than was previously thought.

The Byzantine city was more densely settled than Roman Aelia, as could be assumed on the basis of its especial status in this period as the Holy City of Christianity. In this period, Justinian erected the splendid "Nea" Church (see below, p. 51), the discovery of which has solved an important topographical problem of Byzantine Jerusalem. The current restoration work in the Church of the Holy Sepulchre (then called the "Church of the Anastasis [Resurrection]", a joint effort of various Christian bodies, has gone far to clarify several controversial points: Thus, it was found that around the traditional tomb there had been a row of columns and piers supporting the dome, with open spaces between the piers. The architect Oeckonomopolis was able to expose the edge of the apse of the basilica which had stood to the east of the tomb and part of the stylobate of the eastern row of columns in the court surrounding Golgotha.

The Temple Mount remained abandoned till Omayyad times, when the supporting walls were repaired and adjacent palaces erected, along the Southern and Western Walls — recent discoveries most unexpected.

EXCAVATIONS

The Archaeological Excavations near the Temple Mount

B. Mazar

The archaeological excavations south and southwest of the Temple Mount which have continued without break since 28 February 1968, and will continue for some time to come, are being conducted on behalf of the Israel Exploration Society and the Hebrew University, Jerusalem, under the direction of the author, with the assistance of M. Ben-Dov and a permanent staff of archaeologists and technicians.* The area being uncovered encompasses the upper part of the "Ophel" hill, south of the Temple Mount, as well as the slopes of this spur, in the Tyropoeon and Kidron valleys.

Attention has been focussed upon stratigraphy throughout the area of excavations, in an effort to reveal as clear a picture as possible of the area which, for many generations, was one of the centres of life in Jerusalem.

The Herodian Period

The most decisive developments to take place in the topography of this region are related to Herod's enormous expansion of the Temple Mount by building up the surrounding slopes and valleys on the east and west, levelling the resulting platform, enclosed within mighty supporting walls founded on the very bedrock. According to Josephus, Herod built a Royal Stoa towering over the southern part of the Outer Court, the entire length of the Southern Wall (about 280 m); in his quite detailed description of this building, he states that it "was a structure more noteworthy than any under the sun" (*Antiquities* XV, 412). He also relates of two gates in the Southern Wall, mentioned also in the Mishna: "the two Huldah Gates on the south, that served for coming in and for going out" (Middoth 1:3).

* J. Aviram has been of the greatest assistance as administrative director. Special gratitude is expressed to the Ambassador College of Pasadena, California, for considerable assistance in supporting the excavations.

These gates led to tunnels beneath the Royal Stoa, emerging to the north, the present "Double" and "Triple" Gates (today blocked and as yet incompletely investigated).

Parts of the enormous supporting walls of the Temple Mount are perfectly preserved in their original, Herodian state, especially near the south-eastern and south-western corners; their planning is superb as is the workmanship of the dry masonry. Those portions above the Herodian ground-level were finely finished with smooth, uniform bosses on the huge ashlars, in contrast to the rough, protruding bosses of the subterranean courses, beneath the paved Herodian streets running along the walls.

The upper exterior of the Western and Southern Walls, rising over the level of the Temple Mount, had been ornamented with a row of pilasters with capitals, similar to the exterior of the Herodian structure surrounding the Haram el-Khalil at Hebron. The fragments of capitals, lintels, friezes, panels and other architectural members, are partly from the upper courses of the Walls and from the gates, but mostly from the Royal Stoa. The decoration is in the Herodian style, with a rich corpus of geometrical and floral patterns (no faunal or human motifs have been noted), fitting in well with the known art of this period in Jerusalem.

"Robinson's Arch"

In beginning our excavations, we were aided considerably by the results of the 1867–1870 explorations of Charles Warren around the Temple Mount, which provided some picture of the lay of the bedrock, of the subterranean courses of the Herodian walls, and of the floors, installations, and channels in this region. The width of the arch is 15.50 m; it spanned a paved street and rested upon a large pier built opposite the extant skewback, some

12.40m from it. Warren assumed that this was the first of a series of arches forming a bridge over the Tyropoeon valley, connecting the Temple Mount with the Upper City on the west. This theory has generally been accepted. In our excavations here, we uncovered parts of the street, paved with large, smooth flagstones, which ran southward along the Western Wall between the Wall and the pier of the arch. The pier of the arch was completely revealed; founded upon the bedrock in the typically Herodian manner, it is the same width as "Robinson's Arch" and some 3.60 m thick. It contains four small cells opening upon the paved street; within these were found stoneware, weights, coins (from Agrippa I to the First Jewish Revolt) and Herodian pottery — and we can assume that they served as shops for those coming to the Temple. In subsequent work here, no traces of any other large piers were found to the west. What was found was a series of much smaller piers, progressively shorter as they continued *southwards*. The rubble here also contained numerous stone stairs, including some still joined together; and on the remains of one of the smaller piers, there were two steps, *in situ*.

In this light, we concluded that the smaller arches, together with the huge arch, formed an enormous, monumental stairway, leading from the main street up to a gate in the Western Wall, giving access to the Royal Stoa on the Temple Mount. Josephus (*Antiquities* XV, 410) relates that the southern gate led from the Temple Mount by means of a stairway down to the Tyropoeon valley, from where one could ascend to the Upper City. Indeed, immediately north of the huge pier is a series of stairs leading to a paved street which runs to the west.

The Street and Plaza
South of the Southern Wall
At right angles to the paved street running beneath "Robinson's Arch", another Herodian street branches off, along the Southern Wall; also paved with large, smooth flagstones, it is some 6.40 m wide and leads eastward towards the Huldah Gates. In the western part of this street, between the corner and a small series of stairs which raised the level of the street to the east, we found among the rubble from

the destruction of the Second Temple a large stone hewn in an unusual shape, with a niche set into it; near this niche appears a Hebrew inscription which reads; "To the place of trumpeting..."* This ashlar was most certainly the top cornerstone of the south-western corner of the Temple Mount; this was the site of one of the four defensive towers which, according to Josephus (*War* IV, 582), was built by John of Gischala over the Temple chambers, at a point where a priest would blow a trumpet to usher in the Sabbath.

The paved street with its stairs is preserved for only 11.20 m of its length. In deep soundings here, east of the extant pavement, we found two adjoining rows of small rooms, of approximately equal dimensions, which appear to continue till near the "Double Gate". To the south of the wall bordering the street, a large area paved with flagstones was

* Possibly restored "to declare" at the end, as suggested by Prof. Z. Ben-Hayyim.

discovered, a plaza some 13 m wide, running parallel to the street. The plaza was supported on the south by a solid terrace-wall (some 2.50 m thick) which was deeply founded, apparently on bedrock. A network of drainage channels lay beneath the pavement, leading the runoff to the west, towards the large aqueduct running north to south beneath the main street.

The chronology of this building complex is revealed by the many finds — especially coins, pottery and stoneware — found among the debris. It is clear that the street and plaza went out of use at the time of the destruction of the Second Temple.

The Monumental Stairway before the Huldah Gates

The paved street along the Southern Wall runs up to the Huldah Gates. Near the "Double Gate", a broad, monumental stairway was found in quite good condition; it had led from the Ophel on the south up to the Temple gates. These stairs, apparently some

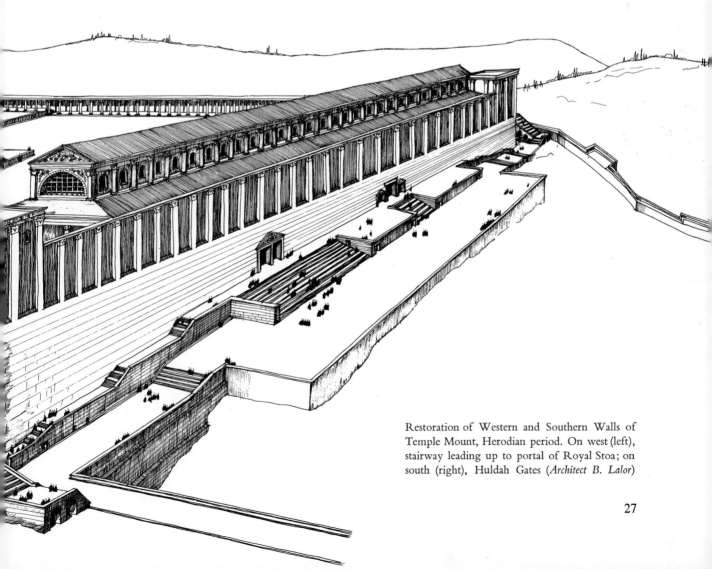

Restoration of Western and Southern Walls of Temple Mount, Herodian period. On west (left), stairway leading up to portal of Royal Stoa; on south (right), Huldah Gates (*Architect B. Lalor*)

Ornamented architectural fragments, Herodian period, found
among debris along Southern Wall

29

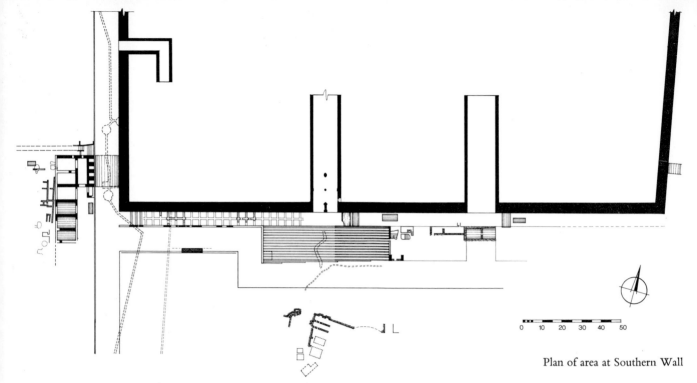

Plan of area at Southern Wall

64 m wide, are founded upon steps cut into the bedrock. South of this stairway we found remains of a plaza paved with smooth flagstones, some 6.50 m lower than the street before the gates.

East of the monumental stairs, between them and the "Triple Gate" and south of the street, we found the remains of a large structure, the plan of which is unclear; what is outstanding in this building is the number of pools and cisterns hewn into the rock and plastered. It may well have been an extensive ritual bath for those coming to the Temple, prior to their entering the holy precincts.

Part of the street was also found before the the "Triple Gate", with the remains of a vault to the south, the same width as the gate (14.70 m). This vault appears to have borne a stairway which led from the plaza up to the street and the gate.

This discovery of the monumental stairs before each of the two gates here raises several problems. It can be assumed that the "stairs" at the Temple Mount, mentioned in the Talmud, may refer to these; for example: "An incident of R. Gamaliel and the elders who were standing at the top of the stairs at the Temple Mount..." (Tosefta, Sanhedrin 2, 2); or "Ben Zoma saw a crowd above the stair at the Temple Mount..." (Babylonian Talmud,

Berachot 58, 1). The allusion here is undoubtedly to a crowd of pilgrims who had gathered on the plaza and ascended the stairs towards the gates. If these passages do refer to the stairs uncovered in our excavations, then the "top of the stairs" here would be the street immediately before the gates. The Mishna notes three courts of law in the Temple precincts: "One used to sit at the gate of the Temple Mount, one used to sit at the gate of the Temple Court, and one used to sit in the Chamber of Hewn Stone" (Sanhedrin 11, 2). The first one probably sat at one of the Huldah Gates, possibly the eastern one, which was used for entering the Temple Mount (Middot 1, 3). We may also note that near the "Triple Gate" we found among the debris many ornamented architectural fragments, including some from the gate itself. The debris also contained a fragment of a stone plaque with a fine frame, similar to that of the "Uzziah epitaph", bearing traces of a skillfully incised Hebrew inscription. Following this discovery, Prof. Y. Yadin brought to my attention a fragment of a Hebrew inscription discovered by de Saulcy over a hundred years ago in this very same place. Much to my surprise, we found that the two are complementary, together forming part of a large monumental inscription, of which only the upper lefthand portion is preserved. The inscription is too fragmentary to enable any true reading.

Section of stairway leading up to Double Gate

SECTION HERODIAN STEPS N — S

719.00
719.00

Left: Fragment of stone plaque with Hebrew inscription, Herodian period, found near Southern Wall; right: drawing of fragment, with joining fragment found by de Saulcy on same site a century ago

Finds from the Herodian Period

The finds of this period, from the various loci — including the cisterns and channels, which went out of use after the destruction of the Second Temple — include large quantities of pottery and stoneware, a large number of coins, glassware (almost all fragmentary) and bone objects. The pottery is almost all of the usual types of this period, known so well from the tombs in Jerusalem and from Qumran, Masada and other sites. The types are mainly the usual functional vessels of local manufacture. Foreign wares, in contrast, are rare. This corpus of pottery, most of which is from the first century C.E., is readily distinguishable from the vessels (especially lamps) of the "Hellenistic" or "Hasmonean" types, found in loci which went out of use as a result of Herod's building projects (as in locus 7038, west of "Robinson's Arch", where the coins were from Antiochus IV till Herod).

A large quantity of stoneware typical of the Herodian period, including ornamented vessels, was found throughout the excavations, especially in the area to the west of the Western Wall. There were numerous types of local wares — from tables and large containers to "measuring cups", small bowls and cups. Some of the vessels are inscribed with private names in Hebrew script, and one fragment bears the Hebrew word *qorban* "sacrifice". There

are also considerable quantities of stone weights: A small group of stone weights bears the Greek letters *LE*, "year 5", and one weight has *LE A*, "year 5, A"; others have the additional word ΒΑCΙΛΕωC. "Of the king", or even ΒΑCΙΛΕωC Α ΦΡ ΜΝΑ, apparently to be understood: "Year 5 of king A, loyal to Caesar. Mina". We are of the opinion that the latter A signifies Agrippa I, which would mean that the weights date from his fifth year (that is 41/42 C.E.), when he gained rule over all Judea and began his extensive projects in Jerusalem, his capital.

Among the finds discovered quite recently is a fragment of a marble plaque, bearing an inscription in early Hebrew script. It was found in locus 4014, in the debris beneath the Omayyad floor of building II, south of the Southern Wall. It measures 9.5 × 10 cm and is 2.5 cm thick. Only middle parts of two lines are preseved, and thus nothing is known of the original size of the plaque, or of the contents of the inscription. The surface of the plaque is well

31

Left: bronze mask; right: bronze figurine depicting Barbarian horseman; both from Aelia Capitolina (2nd century C.E.)

polished and the letters are skilfully incised; the back is rough. This leads to the assumption that the plaque had been fixed in a wall. Dr. Shulamit Gross, of the Geological Institute of the Ministry of Development, has found the stone to be a quite white marble of calcite crystals. It originates in Italy or Greece, and the microtexture is reminiscent of the Carrara marble used in fine sculptures. The extant letters read:

]yr.bn.'[
]y.'[d/g

We may note that the script is lapidary, with dot word-dividers. The inscription is in Hebrew, as indicated by the word *bn*, "son", in the first line, which had undoubtedly been preceded and followed by personal names.

At first, the inscription seemed to us to be uniquely from the late First Temple period, even though the script differs from that usually ascribed to that period. Soon after its discovery, the inscription was shown to Profs. N. Avigad and Y. Yadin, and the latter immediately expressed doubts concerning this dating, and ascribed it to the Second Temple period, comparing the script to that of the Jewish coins. The fact that the plaque was of imported marble also strengthens this latter dating. It could very well be that during the religious-nationalistic reawakening towards the end of the Second Temple period, inscriptions were incised in Jerusalem in the early Hebrew script, as found on the coins, rather than in the square script common in monumental inscriptions of the Herodian period. The dividing dots, positioned high in the line of script, resemble

those in Samaritan inscriptions of the Roman-Byzantine period.

Of the corpus of coins, we should first and foremost note the small number of Hellenistic and Hasmonean copper coins, and the even fewer silver coins — from Ptolemy II to Alexander Janneus; those found are mainly from the area to the west of the Western Wall. In contrast, there were many bronze coins of Alexander Janneus (some 235), which were used also under the Herodian dynasty. A decided majority of the Jerusalem coins are of Herod and his heirs, of all the Roman Procurators, and of the First Jewish Revolt against Rome. We should note that there were relatively few coins of Herod himself and of Archelaus, and that there were many of Agrippa I and of several of the Procurators, especially Coponius and Ambibulus (6–11 C.E.), and Felix (54 and 59 C.E.). Of the coins of the First Jewish Revolt, those of the second year were most plentiful; the first year is represented only by the half-sheqel. No coins of the fifth year were found at all.

Besides the Jerusalem coins (some 1500), there were few foreign coins of the Herodian period, including an imperial issue of Tiberius, in gold, and some silver and copper coins of Tyre and other coastal cities, as well as of the Nabateans.

Between the Two Revolts

Following the destruction of Jerusalem by Titus's legions, in 70 C.E., which entirely depopulated the city, nothing remained in the area of our excavations but the huge supporting walls of the Temple Mount (intact to varying heights), as well as the "Double Gate" and the stairs leading up to it. With the stationing of the Tenth Legion as occupation force in the desolate city, a meagre settlement sprang up on the site; the few remains of channels and floors, mainly in the area of the Herodian street and plaza south of the Mount, may belong to this phase. Of the finds of this period, most noteworthy is a small group of silver and bronze coins, mainly imperial and city issues, from Vespasian to Hadrian, with several of the "Iudaea Capta" type, as well as a number of Nabatean coins (Rabel II), two of Agrippa II, and Bar Kokhba two coins (year 2). The finds of this period also include several decorated lamps of the so-called "Bar Kokhba" type which was so common in Judea at the end of the first

Column fragment bearing Latin inscription mentioning Vespasian and Titus, as well as commander of Tenth Legion

IMPCAESAR
VESPASIANVS
AVG IMPTCAE
SARVESPAVG
L FLAVIVS SILVA
AVG PR PR
LEG X FR

century and the beginning of the second century C.E.

The most interesting discovery was a large fragment of a column found fixed in the foundations of one of the pillars of Omayyad building II, south of the Temple Mount. In the well-preserved Latin inscription, the fifth line had purposely been erased, only the first letter remaining. With minor restorations, the inscription reads: IMP CAESAR/ VESPASIAN[VS] / AVG IMP T C[AE]/SAR VESP AVG/L . . ./AVG PR PR/LEG X FR. The first four lines mention the August Emperor Caesar *Vespasian* (69–79 C.E.) and the August Emperor *Titus* Caesar Vespasian (79–81 C.E.); the three subsequent lines mention the commander of the Tenth Legion Fretensis, whose name has been erased; he was most likely L(ucius) Flavius Silva, who commanded the legion when it was stationed in Jerusalem and was Governor of Provincia Judaea in 73–79/80 C.E.*

Aelia Capitolina

Throughout our excavations, evidence was found of the occupational and public-building activities in the period of Aelia Capitolina, from the days of Hadrian till the end of the third century C.E., and on a much broader scale during the Byzantine period. In erecting their structures and water-installations, the Romans utilized not only the stones which had toppled from the supporting walls of the Temple Mount and those from the buildings and pavements of the Second Temple period, but also newly hewn stone from quarries, located mainly in the area south of the Huldah Gates. The building activities of the Tenth Legion in the area of excavations are evidenced mainly by bricks and roof-tiles, including many bearing this legion's stamps, which were used from the time of Hadrian down to the end of the third century C.E.; other bricks were found stamped "C(olonia) AEL(ia) C(apitolina)". Large quantities of pottery, including many decorated lamps from the second-third centuries C.E., were found throughout the

* See, most recently, W. Eck: *Senatoren von Vespasian bis Hadrian*, Munich, 1970, pp. 98 ff.

33

Herodian pavement and stairs below Southern Wall, with debris from destruction of Second Temple, looking northwest

Hebrew inscription from southwest corner of Temple Mount: "To the place of trumpeting..."

excavations. The number of silver and bronze coins of this period was also large, including city-issues — some from Aelia itself. Of special interest were the finds which were indicative of the importance of the area of our excavations as one of the city's quarters — such as the stone slab (originally a paving stone from the plaza south of the Temple Mount) reused for a monumental inscription in the time of (and dedicated to) Septimius Severus and Caracalla, the text of which concerns the completion of some public project in the Colonia Aelia Capitolina Commodiana.* In several places, we found ornamental architectural members and fragments of Roman marble statuary, as well as artefacts in bronze, gems, seals and similar objects. Of the structures here, which certainly were used by the Tenth Legion, we should note those near the south-western corner of the Temple Mount: In the Roman phase of building 1048, south of the corner, two bronze statuettes were found on the plastered floor,

along with Roman pottery, city coins and many dice; one of the bronzes depicts a barbarian horseman and the other appears to have been of Apollo.

Fragment of monumental inscription in Palaeo-Hebrew script

* This inscription was published by M. Avi-Yonah, apud B. Mazar: *The Excavations in the Old City of Jerusalem, Preliminary Report of the First Season, 1968*, Jerusalem, 1969, pp. 22–24.

Intaglio gems, Roman period

Byzantine Period

Groups of well-preserved buildings were uncovered near both the south-western corner of the Temple Mount and the Turkish wall opposite the "Double Gate", as well as further to the east, near the "Triple Gate".

We may note that in the Early Byzantine period the Christian inhabitants continued to use buildings from the previous period, after thorough renovation and some additions. In this respect, building 7066 south of the pier of "Robinson's Arch" is most illustrative in its later phase: This Early Byzantine house is well preserved, with its arches for supporting the roof, doorways and windows, and many finds — shedding light on an obscure episode in the history of the city. All the coins of this phase of the building are from the time of Constantine and his

Byzantine house (15000) near Triple Gate

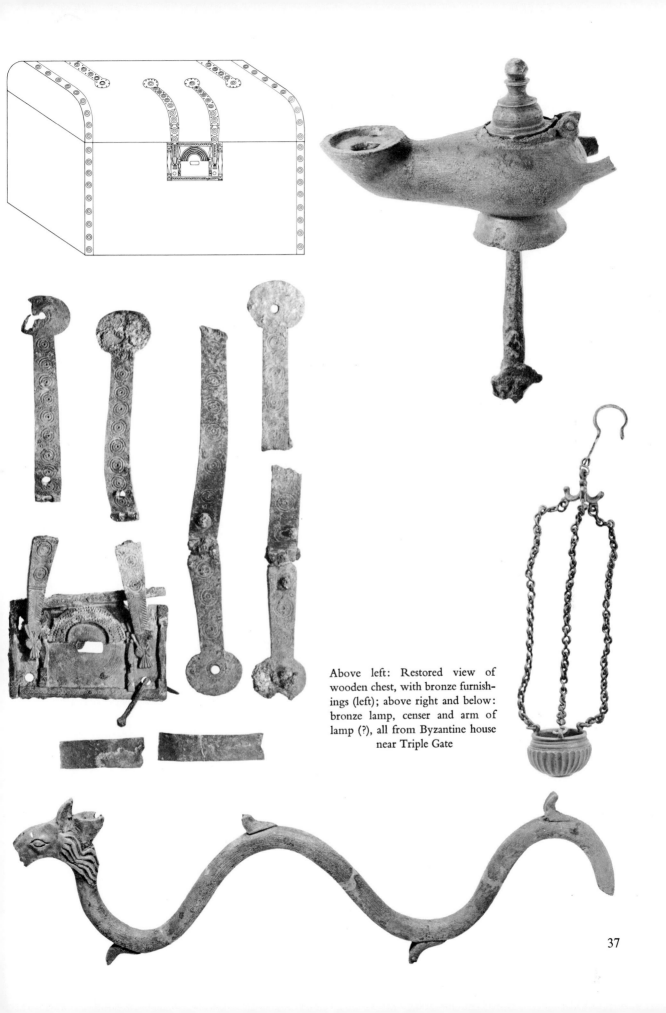

Above left: Restored view of wooden chest, with bronze furnishings (left); above right and below: bronze lamp, censer and arm of lamp (?), all from Byzantine house near Triple Gate

37

Fragment of mosaic floor with inscription, in Byzantine house near stairway to Double Gate

heirs; the five latest coins are of Julian, from the final years of his rule (362–363 C.E.). The layer of rubble and ash in the rooms indicates that the building was destroyed at the end of Julian's reign. The Constantinian structures near the Western Wall may have been destroyed by Jews who, encouraged by Julian, began preparations for the reconstruction of the Temple — which project came to nought upon the emperor's death. Over the ruins of this building and the others in its vicinity, new structures rose in the Late Byzantine period; at the same time, the fine residential quarter in the eastern part of our excavations was further expanded. The residential quarter on the east was enclosed in a solid wall, remains of which have been discovered in considerable stretches on the east and west, some 70 m south of the Southern Wall of the Temple Mount.

As we have noted, the Late Byzantine buildings are well preserved, often to the height of two storeys, with their plastered walls, doorways and windows, pillars with arches, stone and mosaic pavements, cisterns and channels. The decorative architecture (in stone and marble) is interesting, and several types of bricks and roof-tiles are employed, many of them stamped with the names of the craftsmen in Greek, or with trade-marks. Extensive building 15000, currently being excavated near the "Triple Gate", is of two storeys, with

cellars beneath, and includes many rooms and courtyards. It may very well have been a hospice for important pilgrims, possibly built during the stay of the Empress Eudocia in Jerusalem, and undergoing various repairs and modifications in the sixth century C.E. The rich finds of the Late Byzantine period, especially from this last building, leave no doubt that the structures are of the fifth-sixth centuries C.E., and most were destroyed during the Parthian invasion of 614 C.E. At this time, too, the Southern Wall of the Temple Mount was breached, west of the "Double Gate".

A most noteworthy find was made in a Late Byzantine building of two storeys at the southern end of the Herodian stairway near the south-western corner of the Temple Mount. The lintel of the doorway in its northern wall, facing the street, bears a depiction in red paint of two seven-branched *menora*s flanking an incised cross. It is apparent that the painter of the *menora*s disregarded the cross, or even purposely covered it over. Two other *menora*s, flanked by a *shofar* and an *etrog*, are painted in red near the top of the back wall of the entrance hall, flanking a small niche, in this same building. The appearance of Jewish symbols at the entrance to a building which had originally been Christian is somewhat surprising. During the period of Persian domination in Jerusalem, the Persians' Jewish allies here may have taken the building over; at that time, Jewish religio-nationalistic feelings were quite open, and this building is very close to the highly revered Western Wall.

Tombs from the Period of the Judean Monarchy

Throughout our excavations, in debris and fills, much fragmentary pottery from the later period of the First Temple was found mixed with Hellenistic and Herodian sherds or even later material. Such pottery was especially abundant in the fill in one of the soundings beneath the level of the street along the Southern Wall, adjacent to a shaft dug by Warren (where he found a Hebrew seal bearing the name "Haggai son of Shebaniahu"). In the same fill, we found a jar-handle bearing the stamp of "Hoshe'am/Haggai". Among the other finds from the fill were a dozen or so *lamelekh* handles and some bearing the stamped rosette pattern with incised concentric circles; a handle

Byzantine house south of pier of "Robinson's Arch", in Jewish use at end of Byzantine period

bearing the stamp "(belonging) to Naḥum/Has-elyahu"; and a stone weight inscribed *beq'a*, "half" — all from the late First Temple period. In contrast, sherds of the Persian period are scarce (including a handle bearing a "Yehud" stamp, and two Attic sherds).

As a result of Herod's enormous building project, all the earlier remains on the upper "Ophel" and its slopes were totally destroyed; we have as yet found no building remains which can definitely be ascribed to a period prior to Herod. Of the period of the Judean Monarchy, south of the Southern Wall, we have found only two loci which contained material solely of this age: One, a "pocket" in the bedrock east of the "Double Gate", contained a small deposit of seventh century B.C.E., pottery; and the other, the bottom of a plastered hewn cistern, adjacent to the Southern Wall, east of the "Triple Gate", contained a considerable group of

whole and fragmentary vessels, apparently of the eighth century B.C.E.

A different picture is revealed in the area west of the Western Wall. As the excavations progressed in this area, it became more evident that low on the slope of the western hill, opposite the Temple Mount and the "Ophel", there was an extensive necropolis from the First Temple period. Even though the tombs had been hewn into the bedrock, some were destroyed and others were reused for other purposes in later periods, especially in Hero-dian times. In none did any bones or funerary furniture survive, but their character and date are generally clear. Especially interesting are the tombs having a square shaft hewn into the rock, with an entrance leading to a spacious, plastered burial chamber; in the ceiling of the chamber is a sort of rectangular "chimney", probably the *"nefesh"*, which had been sealed from above by slabs of stone.

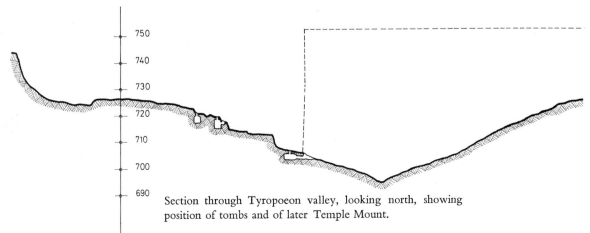

Section through Tyropoeon valley, looking north, showing position of tombs and of later Temple Mount.

Scaraboid seal bearing depiction of griffin, period of Judean monarchy (8th century B.C.E.)

Seal-impression on jar-handle: *Hoshe'am* (*son of*) *Haggai*; found in fill within tomb below Herodian street, along Southern Wall

In one of the tombs of this type there was a niche hewn into the rock of the façade before the chamber, apparently intended for a memorial plaque. This general type of tomb is known in this country from the Phoenician cemetery south of Achzib, dating from the eighth-seventh centuries B. C. E. The foundations of the Western Wall overlay the approaches to two of these tombs on the east, which may have been hewn quite close to the valley bed here.

Another of the tombs, where we found a large deposit of pottery vessels and other articles, was of the mid-eighth to mid-seventh centuries B.C.E. Most of the pottery is certainly earlier than the final stages of the period of the First Temple, and three of the vessels bear private names incised in the Hebrew script of the eighth-seventh centuries B.C.E. — raising the question of how these vessels came to be in the tomb, most of them being preserved intact. It may have been reutilized for storing vessels cleared from the other tombs. Or it may have been cleared at an early date as a storeroom by an inhabitant of the "Mishne" quarter.

This discovery raises numerous questions concerning the necropolis of Jerusalem in the period of the First Temple, and the initiation of settlement in the quarter located on the western hill. Firstly, the practice of clearing tombs in areas newly included within the city proper is known from several ancient sources. Ezekiel heaped his wrath upon the royal tombs close by the holy precincts of the Temple, and called for their removal (Ezekiel 43 : 7–9).

The fact that the kings of Judah were buried in a necropolis other than the royal tombs in the City of David is noteworthy. This burial-ground may have been on the lower slopes of the western hill, opposite the Temple Mount. Later, from the days of King Manasseh on, the royal burial-grounds were located in the "garden of Uzza", probably at the foot of the Mount of Olives near Silwan village. This cemetery was probably removed upon settlement of the western hill, on its eastern slope and in the Valley (the Mishne and "*Makhtesh*"), which gradually grew from the days of Hezekiah on.

Finally, we may note that Bronze Age sherds were found in the brown soil remaining in the crevices of the bedrock in the region of the necropolis, the oldest of them of the Middle Bronze II. This shows that, already early in the second millennium B.C.E., the eastern slope of the western hill, above the Valley, was utilized for agriculture.

I

Upper: Terra sigillata bowl, Herodian period, Citadel excavations. Lower: Herodian pottery painted in "Pseudo-Nabatean" style; excavations adjacent to Temple Mount

II
Mosaic floor, Herodian period, Jewish Quarter excavations, area F

Excavations in the Jewish Quarter of the Old City, 1969–1971

N. Avigad

The Jewish Quarter of the Old City of Jerusalem spreads over the north-eastern part of the Upper City of Second Temple times — the western hill of ancient Jerusalem overlooking the Temple Mount to the east. This is generally thought to have been the upper class residential quarter, containing such important structures as the palace of the Hasmoneans, the palace of Ananias and other such buildings. Till recently it remained something of an archaeological blank-spot.

Large parts of the Jewish Quarter were destroyed during the 1948 War; after the city was reunited in 1967, reconstruction work began with the clearance of the modern ruins. Thus, unforeseen opportunities for systematic excavations arose. In the summer of 1969 our excavations commenced on behalf of the Institute of Archaeology of the Hebrew University, the Israel Exploration Society and the Israel Department of Antiquities and Museums, with the participation of the Jewish Quarter Reconstruction and Development Company.* During the first three seasons of excavation, in 1969-1971, we cleared nine areas (A-K), selected on the basis of reconstruction work about to be carried out.

During the excavations, it became clear that the stratigraphy of the Jewish Quarter, athough well-established, was not uniform at all the sites explored. In several spots, settlement was not continuous in all periods, and the remains of certain periods were found entirely out of context. Here, we can merely review the more important finds from the various periods, and their significance for the study of the city.

* I must thank all those who have supported our project: The America-Israel Cultural Foundation, the Ambassador College of Pasadena, California, and Dr. R. Hecht. The author directed the excavations, assisted by A. Mazar, R. Reich, H. Geva, Dina Kastel, Sara Hofri, D. Bahar, D. Zipper, I. Levi and N. Gershon. Dr. Y. Meshorer has treated the numismatic material.

The Period of the First Temple

The matter of the start of settlement in this section of the city has been a crucial point in archaeological research for many years, and its solution is undoubtedly one of the most important achievements of our excavations. It is now clear that in most of the sites in which we reached the virgin soil overlying bedrock, there were traces of settlement from the Israelite period. This was especially so in areas A, B and F, where considerable construction remains were found, dating to the 8th-7th centuries B.C.E.

In area A, we may note especially a long structure, between the walls of which was a fill of red earth. This is the substructure of a building overlying it, of which only floor fragments have been found. The building is oriented on an east-west axis. It has been cut into by a massive city-wall (see below). On the basis of the associated pottery, this building can be ascribed to the 8th century B.C.E.

Most of the other Israelite remains in this site are little more than wall and floor fragments; a rectangular installation hewn into the bedrock, with a round sump in its floor, probably had some agricultural function.

In area B, a wall running north-south, 11 metres long, 1.20 metres wide and 2–3 m high, terminates on the south in a towerlike projection, the corner of

Iron Age II pottery

Segment of Israelite city-wall (late 8th or 7th century B.C.E.), looking north

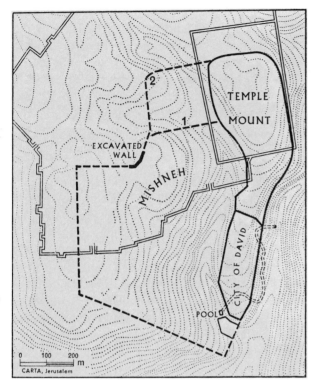

Suggested course (with alternatives 1, 2) of Israelite city-wall on western hill

which is built of large stones laid as headers and stretchers. It is founded upon bedrock and adjoins layers of red soil containing pottery of the Iron Age II. Such pottery was also found between the stones of the wall when a portion of it was dismantled.

In area F, three natural terraces were uncovered; in the middle terrace we found relatively many remains of the Israelite period: wall fragments (in which two building phases were apparent) and floors, well-preserved. The layers of earth covering these early remains contained large quantities of Israelite pottery from the late 8th and early 7th centuries B.C.E.

Of the smaller finds from the Israelite strata in the various areas, we may point out the pottery figurines of a type commonly found on sites of this period in Judah — the pillar-figurines of women holding their breasts, clearly a fertility symbol (one of our examples is especially expressive) and fragments of animal figurines.

The epigraphical material includes mainly store-jar handles stamped with the various types of royal (*lamelekh*) stamps: with the two-winged and four-winged varieties, bearing the names of the towns of Hebron, Ziph and *mmšt*. Two impressions of private seals have also been found: "Belonging to Ṣaphan (son of) Abima'aṣ" and "Belonging to Menahem (son of) Yobanah". Of special interest is a store-jar fragment bearing a three-line ink inscription in fine Hebrew script. The first two lines seem to have contained names, only one of which, Mikhayahu, is clearly legible. In the third line, there is the word *qn'rṣ*, which apparently should be restored to read [*El*] *qoneh areṣ*. This phrase appears also in the 8th century B.C.E. Phoenician inscription from Karatepe: *b'lšmm w'lqnrṣ*, "Baalshamem and El-the-Creator-of-the-Earth". We may compare this with Genesis 14; 19: *El Elyon qoneh šamayim we'areṣ*, "The most high God, creator of heaven and earth". We can assume that this vessel may have been intended for offerings to be brought to the Temple, only a short distance away.

All this is surely sufficient evidence to indicate that there was a settlement on the western hill of Jerusalem during the First Temple period. Previously this had been assumed tentatively on the basis of meagre pottery evidence from the excavations in the Jerusalem Citadel (David's Tower), in the Armenian Garden and, recently, on Mount Zion (for the latter, see below, pp. 57 ff.; see also pp. 7 f.). The first definite evidence for a walled Israelite settlement on the western hill is the section of city-wall discovered in the Israelite stratum in area A: This wall is 7 metres thick, and so far some 40 metres of its length have been uncovered (see p. 44). It is built entirely of large stones, both dressed and rough, laid with no binding. Two to seven courses have been preserved, to a maximum height of 3.30 metres. This, however, is merely the foundation of the wall, overlying the bedrock. On either side of the wall we found a deposit of earth which contained Iron Age II pottery. Only at the northern part of the

Seal-impression: "*Belonging to Ṣaphan (son of) A/bima'aṣ*"; Israelite period

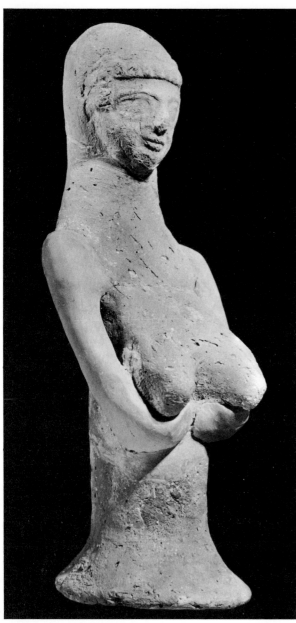

Fertility figurine, Israelite period

southern end of the exposed portion, it turns sharply to the west, possibly forming a tower. It is at this spot that the wall cuts through the Israelite building mentioned above. The portion of the house which remains is on the west, outside the line of the wall, and thus we can conclude that the western hill was at first an unwalled quarter (8th century B.C.E.), and only later (in the latter part of that century or in the 7th century B.C.E.) part of it was included within the fortifications.

That Jerusalem had spread beyond the city-walls in the period of the First Temple is hinted at already in the Bible, where mention is made of two suburbs, the *Mishne*, and the *Makhtesh* (Zeph. 1 : 10–11; and cf. Neh. 11 : 9) — which the Commentaries definitely regarded as outside the walls. And now, the present findings are decisive in solving the longstanding historical-topographical controversy surrounding the spread of the city to the western hill in this period. A new question rises, however: Exactly when and by whom was the newly-discovered wall built? The Bible mentions various kings as the builders or restorers of the walls of Jerusalem during the period which would suit the archaeological evidence: Hezekiah, his son Manasseh, and Josiah. In our opinion there are reasonable grounds for ascribing the building of this wall to Hezekiah, who 'built up all the wall that was broken, and raised it up to the towers, and *another wall without*" (2 Chron. 32 : 5). Tentatively, we can assume that the wall which we discovered ran southward, turned towards the wall of the City of David and joined it in a manner which included the Siloam pool within the fortified city. Admittedly, this suggested course for the wall involves certain topographical difficulties, and variant solutions are possible (in all of which, however, the Siloam pool must be included within the walls).

The Period of the Second Temple

After the destruction of Jerusalem by the Babylonians in 586 B.C.E., the western hill seems to have been abandoned. In any event, except for a few isolated sherds, we found nothing in our excavations from the period of the Return from Exile and the Persian period. It is more difficult to explain the absence of remains from the early Hellenistic period, except in fills, where some pottery of this period was found. Most noteworthy are several *Yehud*

wall were there some stones of its upper, exposed part. On the eastern side of the wall, a fragment of crushed-lime floor was preserved, in one place overlying even the stones of the wall. This may have been the entrance to a room within the wall. The floor is of special stratigraphic importance, for it is built over fill containing Israelite pottery, and the pottery found above is also from this same period.

This section of city-wall runs some 275 metres west of the Temple Mount, and its general direction is oriented from northeast to southwest. At the seal-impressions, with the *ṭet*-symbol, and several *yršlm* (=Jerusalem) seal-impressions, which are now generally ascribed to the Hellenistic period.

In contrast, it was found that extensive building activities subsequent to the Israelite period took place at the end of the Hasmonean period. Thus, for instance, we found the remains of a Hasmonean building directly overlying the Israelite city-wall. Nearby were the massive foundations of a square building, in the nature of a fortress. The dating of the structures of this period and the subsequent ones is greatly facilitated by the numismatic finds, which generally are quite abundant.

The most active period as far as building was concerned was the time of the Herodian dynasty. Remains from this period are found in almost every spot. One house, from the end of the Hasmonean period and the beginning of Herod's reign (first century B.C.E.) should be described in detail: In site E we found the remains of a spacious dwelling which apparently belonged to a wealthy family. The entire plan of the dwelling was preserved, spreading over an area of some 200 square metres and comprising a series of rooms and corridors, with an inner court; the latter included a large reservoir with steps leading down into it. The walls were generally preserved to a metre in height. In the western wall of the house, preserved to 1.40 metres above the floor, there had been wall cupboards in niches, in which we found much pottery.

The pottery from the house is typical of the assemblage known for the first centuries B.C.E. and C.E., including a group of wine-jars (some with Latin inscriptions), imported from Italy in the first century B.C.E. The occupants of the house also used luxury ware of the important Eastern *terra sigillata* type, also ascribed to the same century. The lamps discovered in this house are mainly of two types, both common under the Hasmoneans and continuing in use into the Herodian period; one common type, the so-called "Herodian lamp", with spatulated nozzle, was entirely lacking. This would appear to indicate that the type had not yet come into use at an early stage of Herod's reign. It may have made its appearance only in the middle of his reign or even later.

The house's foundations rest upon bedrock though in part they overlie foundations of older structures. The fill contains pottery identical to that

Lamps from Herodian dwelling; 1st century B.C.E. (site E)

above the floor levels. Beneath one of the rooms was a blocked cistern from the 2nd century B.C.E. The building can be dated more precisely on a numismatic basis, for on and beneath the floors, bronze coins came to light by the hundreds. Those found above the floors were mostly from the Hasmonean period and some from the first years of Herod's reign. In the fill beneath the floors, only Hasmonean coins were found, leading to the conclusion that the house was built in the first half of the first century B.C.E. The house went out of use towards the end of the first century B.C.E. — apparently in the middle of Herod's reign.

After the building had been destroyed, late in Herod's reign or later, a street was built over its ruins, paved with especially large slabs of stone. This pavement, spreading westward, was uncovered for a stretch of about 50 metres, mainly in area K, and seems to have been one of the main streets of the quarter, leading from west to east towards the Temple Mount. For its entire length it overlies building remains resting at the same level as the dwelling described above.

Of the remains uncovered beneath the paved street, there was a group of cisterns and stepped baths: In one of the latter we found a heap of waste material from a glass workshop, including large quantities of glass fragments from the first century B.C.E. Glass fragments distorted by heat, lumps of glass and slag indicate the presence of a local industry. This discovery is of prime importance for the history of technology of the glass industry, for this is the earliest instance of moulded vessels being found together with vessels manufactured by the blowing technique. On the basis of this discovery, which is in a clear stratigraphic context, it is possible to place the invention of glass-blowing in the mid-first century B.C.E.

In the lower terrace in area F, we uncovered the remains of a house of the Herodian period which was destroyed at the time of the destruction of Jerusalem in 70 C.E. This appears to have been a wealthy home or a public building, and we were able to discern at least two building phases. Two rooms were uncovered, one paved with a fine mosaic floor, with geometric patterns in black and red (see Pl. II). The significance of this mosaic lies in the fact that it is the first mosaic in Jerusalem which can be ascribed to the period of the Second Temple. Other mosaic pavements of this period have been found at Masada and, indeed, the patterns there are in part identical.

In area B, some 150 metres west of the Temple Mount, we uncovered the remains of a house of some 55 square metres. It contained an entrance room, four rooms, a small kitchen and a bath. The walls were preserved to an average height of a metre above the floor-level. The rooms seem to have formed the basement of a house, the upper floor of

Terra sigillata jug from Herodian dwelling (site E)

which no trace remains. This house was destroyed by an intense fire and was filled with fallen stones, wooden beams (carbonized) and layers of ash. The plastered walls were completely covered with soot, and the debris concealed many artefacts. What is unique here is the fact that the debris had not been cleared away or disturbed by later construction: Everything remained just as it was when the building was destroyed. The numerous coins which came to light in its rooms are all of the first century C.E., and most are of the First Revolt (that is, 67–69 C.E.). Thus, the house was destroyed during the destruction of Jerusalem at the hands of the Romans, in 70 C.E.

The objects found in the three main rooms were scattered over the floors; in several places the fragments were found in heaps. These were storage vessels, utensils, furniture and coins. Of the pottery, we may note store-jars, cooking-pots, flasks, juglets and small scent-bottles (some also in glass) — all of types common in the first century C.E. Especially noteworthy are the many stone objects: large vases on high feet, turned on some lathe-like apparatus; small bowls of similar manufacture; mortars and grinding stones of basalt; a set of measuring vessels; and a series of weights. Some of these are quite rare, but most are of the known repertory of the first century C.E.

In the corner of one of the rooms an iron spear

Herodian dwelling (site E)

was found leaning against the wall as if left ready for use, and against a wall in the small kitchen, we found the skeletal arm of a young woman who apparently did not manage to escape when the house went up in flames, collapsing upon her. This was the sole instance of human remains left from the disaster which overtook the house. One of the stone weights bears the Aramaic inscription "[Of] Bar Kathros"; the Talmud mentions Kathros as the name of one of the four High Priestly families who abused their status in granting their kin positions in the Temple, exploting the people (cf. Pesahim 57:1).

* * *

In the realm of art and architecture of the period of the Second Temple, we can point to several impressive finds, which open new vistas in our knowledge of these crafts in Jerusalem.

Relief with cornucopiae. In the debris above a floor ascribed to the first century C.E., we found a fragment of a limestone tablet, 14 centimetres long and 10 centimetres thick, carved on its narrow side. The relief is seemingly part of a frieze of metopes, this being the only extant metope. On either side of the metope there are plain stripes and an astragal pattern ("bead and reel"). Within the metope, two crossed cornucopiae are respresented, tied with a ribbon. Between the two horns is a pomegranate on a stem, from which spout leaves. The workmanship is fine. This relief is assumed to have been part of a stone table.

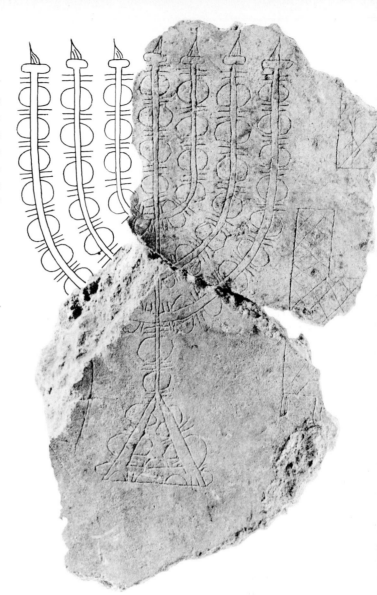

Incised *menorah* design (with reconstruction)

Relief metope depicting double cornucopiae with pomegranate

48   Above: large stone vessel from "Burnt House" (site B); below: stone table with ornamented edge

Till now, the motif of crossed cornucopiae with pomegranate has been known only on Hasmonean coins; but this is the first instance that this specifically Hasmonean motif appears on an object other than a coin.

Fresco fragments. Within the fill between two floors in area A, we found many fragments of painted plaster (frescoes), surprisingly colourful and pleasantly patterned (see Pl. III). The fragments came from the ruins of some other structure, apparently a splendid building from the time of Herod (37–4 B.C.E.), at latest, as is evidenced by the coins of Alexander Janneus and Herod found with the fragments.

The use of frescoes in the buildings of Herod is known from other sites excavated in this country, such as Masada. The frescoes found in Jerusalem, however, are notable for their diversity of motifs and in the fine workmanship of the painting. Besides the painted panelling and the conventional imitation of marble, we find as typical such motifs as bunches of fruits (pomegranates and apples) and leaves in an impressionistic style, witness of a high standard of painting. We should especially note the employment of architectural motifs, such as three-dimensional paintings of dentils, previously unknown in this country.

Grafitto of a menorah. Of extreme interest is the depiction of a seven-branched candelbrum (*menorah*), incised on two fragments of unpainted plaster, found among the fragments of fresco. The three left-hand branches are missing. The depiction is 20 centimetres high. The triangular base, the short stem and the branches (taller than in most ancient depictions) are most noteworthy. All the elements of the *menorah* (including the base!) are ornamented with a motif of knops separated by two parallel lines — a schematic astragal pattern.

Depictions of the *menorah* in the period of the Second Temple are most rare. The *menorah* on the coins of Mattathias Antigonus, last of the Hasmonean kings (40–37 B. C. E.), are miniscule and schematic; the *menorah* motif appearing repeatedly in Jason's Tomb in Jerusalem (late first century B.C.E. or early first century C.E.) is merely a hurried sketch. The detailed depiction on the Arch of Titus in Rome was carved some time after the

Impression of Roman intaglio gem, depicting Hermes

destruction of the Second Temple, and the ornamented base there is often thought not to reflect the base of the *menorah* as it had been in Jerusalem.

It would thus appear that the depiction from the Jewish Quarter excavations is the earliest detailed depiction of the *menorah* which stood in the Temple. It was incised into the plaster as a symbolic ornament at a time when the original object was located some hundreds of metres away, in the Temple.

Architectural fragments. As for architecture, we may note, foremost, the fine capital found in area C in the stratum ascribed to the first century C.E. Made of local limestone in the Corinthian style, it differs from the usual type in its stylized form and in the smooth leaves. This unique capital is a masterpiece of architectural stone-carving. It is identical stylistically with the capitals carved on the façade on the Tomb of Queen Helena in Jerusalem,

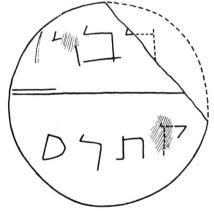

Stone weight, inscribed with name of Kathros family in Hebrew script

Corinthian capital, 1st century C.E. (site C)

Column base in Attic style (site C); height of original column, about 12 m.

Ionic capital and column segment in Hellenistic style, as found (site H)

though the execution here is finer and more delicate. Another capital of unusual size, in Ionic style, was found in site H, in an unstratified context, along with several column drums and an Attic column base. This capital, too, is outstanding in its workmanship, in the pure, Hellenistic style. The height of its column may have reached ca. 10 m. Parallels to this capital are found in the large Hellenistic temples in Asia Minor. We may note that imitations of this style capital can be seen at the top of the engaged columns on the façade of "Zachariah's Tomb" in the Kidron valley. Another architectural surprise came to light in area C: Beneath a floor ascribed to the end of Herod's reign, there was a huge column base, with a lower diameter of 1.80 metres. Its profile is in the Attic style, and the execution is most precise. On the basis of the conventional proportions, this was the base of a column at least 12 metres high.

The Period following the Destruction of the Second Temple

Of the Roman period, following the destruction of the Second Temple, we have found in our excavations in the Jewish Quarter a single, rather meagre stratum, spread over a fairly wide area. The building remains are few, mainly numerous roof-tiles stamped with the symbols or name of the Tenth Legion *Fretensis*, evidence that this legion of the Roman army was stationed here. Of the Roman city which rose over the ruins — Aelia Capitolina — we have found no traces here. This is so of most of the areas where we excavated, except possibly at area G, where the finds have not yet been examined sufficiently.

In most of our sites no Byzantine stratum was found, either; however, remains of public buildings of this period were found in two sites:

The bath-house.

In the uppermost stratum in site C, we uncovered the remains of a Byzantine bathhouse. The extant portions include mostly the substructure of the building and a broad courtyard, paved with flagstones. The building was uncovered for only 17 metres of its length and 5.6 metres of its width. It is built of ashlars and contains three hypocausts, arranged in a row from south to north. These latter, which heated the bathing rooms above, are built with numerous pillars and vaults made of thin bricks, thoroughly sooted from the fire and smoke. Above the southernmost hypocaust was the *caldarium*, or steam-bath. Here there were benches built against the walls and a sitting-bath, all built of brick faced with marble slabs. In another room we found an elongated bathtub, also faced with marble. The inner side of the walls were faced with a layer of square ceramic flue-pipes which channeled hot air from below, warming the rooms. Two Arab lamps were discovered within the hypocaust, and there were traces of later walls in the paved courtyard, indicating that the bathhouse continued to be used well into the Early Arab period.

The "Nea" Church.

In area D we discovered a section of massive masonry, some 13.70 metres long, 6.5 metres wide and 8 metres high. This is founded upon bedrock and is constructed of large stones on the exterior (east), and smaller stones within. The wall runs from north to south and contains an apse 5 metres in diameter, pointing east. West of the thick wall, within the building, are remains of two additional walls, one perpendicular to the massive wall and the other parallel to it. Local conditions prevented extension of the excavation area, but there is no doubt that these are the foundations of an enormous church with three apses of which we have uncovered only the smaller southern one. The massiveness of the wall and the location of the building would lead us to believe, on the basis of early pilgrims' descriptions and following the depiction in the Medeba mosaic map, that this was the famous New (Greek: *Nea*) Church of the Theotokos. The "Nea" was built by Justinian in 543 C.E. and destroyed in an earthquake in the 8th century C.E. Its construction and dimensions are related in detail by the contemporaneous historian Procopius.

Excavations in the Jerusalem Citadel

R. Amiran and A. Eitan

The first archaeological excavations in the courtyard of the Citadel near the Jaffa Gate in Jerusalem took place in 1934–1948, under the direction of C. N. Johns, on behalf of the Mandatory Department of Antiquities. In these excavations, a part of the "First Wall" from the period of the Second Temple, which defended the north-western edge of the city, was revealed. Johns, who excavated mainly on the outer side of the wall, distinguished three building phases: the Early Hellenistic period; the Hasmonean period; and the time of Herod. This part of the wall includes the Phasael Tower, one of the three towers built by

Herod at this corner of the city. This impressive tower, the remains of which still reach a considerable height, has been called "David's Tower" since medieval times. In the years 1968–1969, the two authors

Above: Late Israelite seal (impression): *"Belonging to Matanyahu (son of) ʿAzaryahu"*; below: seal-impression on jar-handle, late Persian or early Hellenistic period, depicting pentacle with Hebrew letters between points: "Jerusalem"

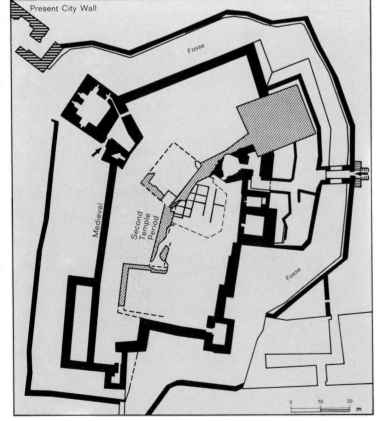

The Citadel, with excavation area in courtyard

Blocked doorway of Hasmonean dwelling

conducted excavations in the courtyard of the Citadel in areas complementing Johns efforts.*

First Temple Period

One of the central questions of historical research in Jerusalem is whether the city spread, in the period of the First Temple, over the western hill (see above and below, pp. 41 ff. and 53). Our excavations have revealed that on the rock surface, some 10–11 metres beneath the surface of the Citadel courtyard, there is an Israelite occupational stratum of the 7th century B.C.E., of a thickness of 1.5 metres.

This evidence, that from Johns' excavations in this area, and that from the excavations undertaken by Miss Kenyon and Tushingham in the Armenian Garden, south of the Citadel, all clearly point to the existence of an Israelite settlement on the western hill during the latter part of the period of the First Temple. (The excavations recently undertaken by Prof. N. Avigad in the Jewish Quarter of the Old City also confirm this conclusion.) Only further excavation, however, can clarify whether or not the western hill was included within the walled area of the city.

* The excavations were directed by the authors on behalf of the Israel Museum, the Israel Exploration Society and the Hebrew University, Jerusalem, with the support of the Jerusalem Municipality.

Of the finds of this period, we may note a small carnelian seal bearing a name in pleasing early Hebrew script: *lmtnyhw 'zryhw*, "Belonging to Matanyahu (son of) 'Azaryahu".

Hasmonean Period

Along the inner line of the Hasmonean wall, we uncovered a massive tower jutting inward from the wall. It is preserved to the height of some 3 metres, and is more than 10 metres long. Several large rooms, of one or more buildings, abut the city-wall and the tower. The walls are preserved to the height of 2.5–3 metres and, in one case, a complete doorway is preserved with lintel intact. Both the two earlier building phases of the city-wall distinguished by Johns belong to this stratum. An important find from this period is a stone mould for casting coin flans. The depressions in the mould are arranged in long, parallel rows; between the depressions in each row are connecting grooves. The importance of this mould lies mainly in the fact that it is the only one

General view of excavations, showing Hasmonean tower (arrow) jutting out from Herodian foundations

of its type which can be ascribed more or less accurately to the final period of the Hasmonean dynasty, the reign of Mattathias Antigonus (40–37 B.C.E.).

Herodian Period

During the reign of Herod this site saw extensive building activities, part of that king's overall building projects. The structures which we uncovered here were built on a huge podium which raised the surface by some 3–4 metres above the level of the previous period. The internal structure of this podium is of interest: There is a network of massive stone walls, 1 metre thick and 3–4 metres high; the spaces between these foundations were filled with enormous quantities of earth and stones. This filled-in network of walls served a dual purpose: On the one hand it served to stabilize the fill and thus strengthen the podium as a whole; on the other hand, the walls seem to have served as foundations for the structures which rose above the podium (see below, pp. 55 ff.). The buildings, on either side of a street, stand three courses high, with floors of flagstones or beaten earth. Many fragments of painted plaster were found fallen on the floor. These buildings seem to have been destroyed during the razing of Jerusalem in 70 C.E.

Josephus speaks of the nature of this area under Herod (*War* II, 17; V, 4–5), relating that the king's palace stood here. It can be assumed that the podium and the buildings standing upon it were part of the palace complex. Above this, fragmentary building remains from the Roman-Byzantine period were uncovered (including a tile pipe bearing stamp-impressions of the Tenth Legion).

Clay sealing depicting Olympian Zeus;
Citadel excavations, Roman period

54

Excavations in the Armenian Garden

D. Bahat and M. Broshi

South of the Citadel of Jerusalem (David's Tower), there stood in ancient times two palaces, according to the early sources: Herod's palace, and that of the Crusader kings of Jerusalem. The present authors spent much of 1971 in excavating in this area, some 125 metres south of the Citadel, uncovering remains of both of these palaces.*

Herod's palace. Josephus relates of Herod's palace here: "Now as these towers were themselves on the north side of the wall, the king had a palace inwardly thereto adjoined, which exceeds all my ability to describe it... entirely walled about to the height of thirty cubits, and adorned with towers at equal distances, and with large bed-chambers... Their roofs were also wonderful, both for the length of the beams, and the splendour of their ornaments. The number of the rooms was also very great... There were besides many porticoes, one beyond another, round about, and in each of those porticoes curious pillars; yet were all the courts that were exposed to the air everywhere green. There were, moreover, several groves of trees, and long walks through them, with deep canals, and cisterns, that in several parts were filled with brazen statues, through which the water ran out... But indeed, it is not possible to give a complete description of these palaces" (*War* V, 4, 4).

We subscribe to the view that, after Herod Archelaus was deposed (in 6 C.E.), the palace was made the seat of the Roman procurator while in Jerusalem, and that it was also the location of the praetorium — the location of the judg-

* The excavations were directed by D. Bahat (November 1970-May 1971) and M. Broshi (June-September 1971), assisted by M. Ben-Ari, S. Eldar and M. Sofer, on behalf of the Armenian Patriarchate and the Department of Antiquities and Museums, and supported by the Samuel H. Kress Foundation through the Jerusalem Fund.

ment and sentencing of Jesus (see below, pp. 87 ff.).

In building this palace, Herod resorted to the same methods employed in the construction of the Temple enclosure: raising the area and leveling it off by means of a huge podium. The platform thus created spread from the Citadel on the north, along the Turkish wall on the west and to the south The eastern limits of the platform are as yet unknown, for the area to the east (in the present compound of the Armenian Patriarchate and to its east) is densely built-up and cannot be investigated. This platform extended over an area of about 300–350 metres from north to south, and some 60 metres, at least, from west to east.* The enormous

* The platform seems to have been about 130 metres wide (see below, pp. 58 f.); if so, it would measure about 400–1000 Herodian feet. For the Herodian foot, see R. Grafman, *IEJ* 20 (1970), pp. 60–66.

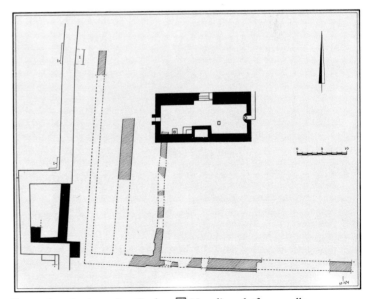

Excavations in Armenian Garden. ▨ Herodian platform walls; ■ southern wing of Crusader palace; ☐ Turkish city-wall; I — traces of Hasmonean "First Wall"

Within Crusader palace, looking east

"Cross of Lorraine" in cistern beneath Crusader palace

B.C.E.), as is indicated by the numerous small finds from this period; store-jar handles bearing the royal *lamelekh* stamp, figurines and many sherds. The several Herodian sherds found within the fill are sure evidence for its proper date.

As noted, the western limits of the platform are at the Turkish city-wall. When we made trial trenches on either side of the city-wall, we discovered beneath the Ottoman courses the lower courses of the city-wall of the Second Temple period — Josephus' "First Wall" (see above, p. 11). The width of this stretch of wall, which is a continuation of that found by C.N. Johns in the courtyard of the Citadel, is twice that of the Turkish wall.

The Crusader palace. Initially, the Crusader kings of Jerusalem resided in the el-Aqṣa and, only after 1118 C.E. did they build their palace south of the Citadel. They selected the site of Herod's palace, though we can assume that they did not realize this fact; but the same reasoning must have led them here: proximity to the Citadel (thus, for instance, Queen Millicent was besieged in the Citadel in 1152 C.E. by her son Baldwin III).

The Crusader builders worked well, founding their walls on bedrock; unfortunately this removed all traces of earlier periods. Besides the supporting walls mentioned above, which might be the foundations of Herod's palace, we found not even one course of the superstructure of the earlier building. Nor did we find any building remains from Roman Jerusalem, though this was the site of the camp of the Tenth Legion — the occupation force in Aelia Capitolina. Of the Byzantine and Early Arab periods, too, nothing concrete was found.

We revealed the ground-floor of the southern wing of the Crusader palace, including two vaulted halls, 17 metres long. These seem to have served as stores for foodstuffs. Beneath the halls there are enormous hewn cisterns. On the rock wall of one of them is a Patriarchal cross (Cross of Anjou, today known as the Cross of Lorraine), in relief.

The Crusader city-wall seems also to have run on the same line as the Turkish wall, continuing along the ridge above the Gehenna valley. In one of the towers of the Turkish wall, we uncovered the remains of a Crusader tower.

quantities of earth fill were stabilized by a network of supporting walls, four of which were revealed in our excavations. Of the superstructure of the palace, nothing has been found — neither in our excavations and in those in the Citadel to the north (see above, p. 54), nor in Kathleen Kenyon's area L, south of the platform. The fill of the platform had been taken from strata of the Israelite IIC period (7th century

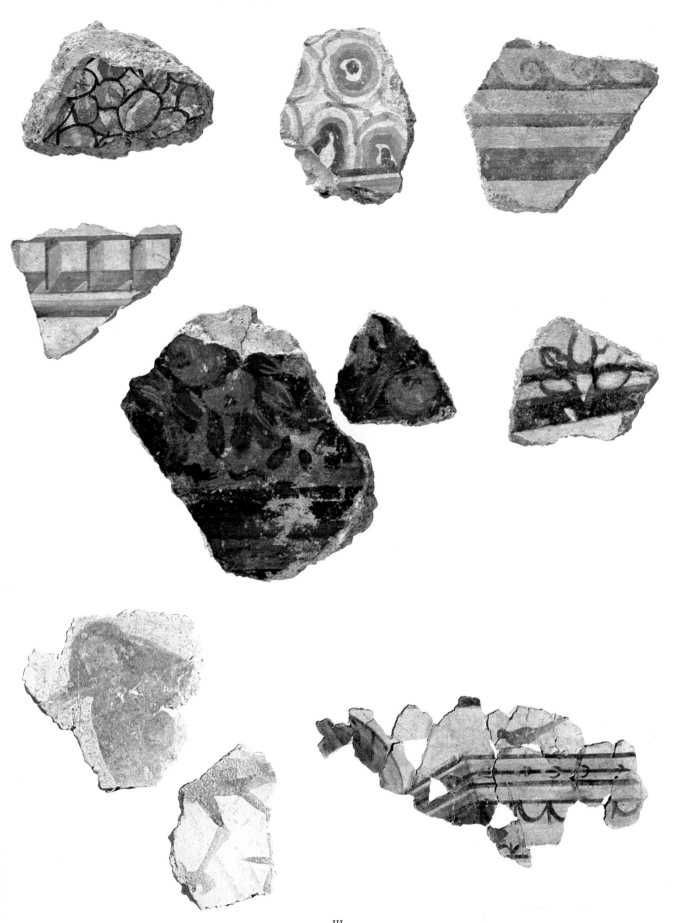

III

Fresco fragments, Herodian period (two upper rows, Jewish Quarter excavations; lower row, Mount Zion excavations)

Excavations in the House of Caiaphas, Mount Zion

M. Broshi

Between July 1971 and December 1972, excavations were conducted in the courtyard of the Armenian Monastery of St. Saviour, built around the house ascribed to the High Priest Caiaphas, just outside the Zion Gate.*

Israelite period. In every spot where we approached bedrock, typical Israelite remains were found, especially pottery and figurines (human and animal images), indicating that this location was settled already in the 7th century B.C.E. Unlike at the nearby site in the Armenian Garden, it is clear that the finds here were in context and not part of a fill. We encountered few actual building remains from this period, including one house, and it would seem that the builders of the period of the Second Temple destroyed most of the earlier building here. It is still impossible to say whether the summit of Mount Zion had been included within the walled city of the First Temple period, and whether the "broad wall" (see above, pp. 41 ff.) also encompassed this part of the city.

The Persian period. Several finds of the Persian period (4th century B.C.E.) were discovered out of stratigraphical context, including two handles bearing seal-impressions with the word *Yhd*, in early Hebrew script (this was the name of the district of Judah in Persian times), and a small silver coin bearing the same name. We do not know the source or significance of these finds, for the city of this period seems to have been limited to the area of the Lower City, to the east. The coin is of special interest: Since the time when the late E. L. Sukenik

identified the first Jewish coin of this type, some 40 years ago, more than twenty such coins, of some seven types, have been published, but so far only two of them originate in scientific excavations, both in Jerusalem.

Late Second Temple period. After a considerable gap, settlement was renewed on the site in the first century B.C.E., apparently around the eve of Herod's accession. We have uncovered many remains from this period, the finest and best preserved in our excavations: houses with rooms preserved up to their roofs, courts and water installations. It would seem that the Herodian structures in the western part of our excavations were of a different character: The walls were quite thick (up to 1.6 metres), and they may be from some public building. Of the two phases found in this area, the earlier structures seem to have been

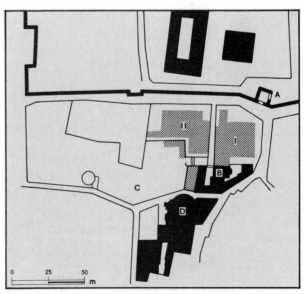

Excavations on Mount Zion. I–II — excavation areas; A — Zion Gate; B — "House of Caiaphas"; C — Armenian cemetery; D — Church of the Dormition

* The excavations are being directed by the author, in association with E. Netzer (architect) and Mrs. Yael Yisraeli, on behalf of the Armenian Patriarchate and the Department of Antiquities and Museums. The Samuel H. Kress Foundation of New York is assisting the project, through the Jerusalem Fund.

General view of excavation area I, looking southwest

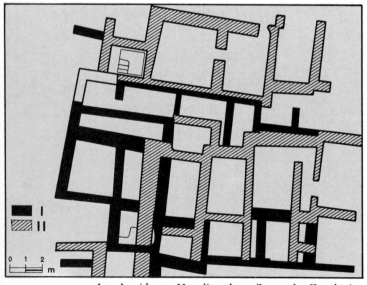

Area I, with two Herodian phases (I — early; II — late)

destroyed by an earthquake, and the later builders did not regard them as sufficiently stable, preferring to build their walls adjacent and parallel to the older ones, set off some tens of centimetres. The earthquake was probably that of 31 B.C.E., which Josephus relates as having brought about much destruction and loss of life.

As in other sites excavated in Jerusalem, the water installations here are quite numerous — cisterns, pools and baths — some rock-hewn and some constructed, and all vaulted over. This region was densely populated, and the houses here were certainly of two storeys, some even of three. There are large quantities of small finds, especially pottery. Some rare and unexpected objects also came to light, such as a sword preserved together with its wooden sheath, most probably remaining from the last battle in the Upper City.

The finest finds from this period are, without doubt, the fresco fragments; some were found *in situ* and most in fills (Pl. III). These were entirely unexpected, for this is the first time that frescoes of this period were found in this country, containing animal motifs: birds on a stylized architectural-floral background of trees, wreaths, buildings and the like. Frescoes of this period are known on several sites — Masada, Herodium, Jericho (Tulul Abu el-'Alaiq), Samaria and Caesarea — but in all these the motifs are geometrical or imitative of coloured marble. Recently, splendid fragments of frescoes of this period were found in the excavations in the Jewish Quarter of Jerusalem, and there the style is somewhat more realistic (see above, p. 49). Nor are animal motifs found on the hundreds of ornamental Jewish ossuraries from Jerusalem from this period. It would appear that, in the splendid private homes at the summit of the Upper City, the wealthy allowed themselves to be lax in the prohibition against graven images.

Byzantine period. The "Church of St. Sion", which stood adjacent to the site of our excavations — approximately beneath the present Church of the Dormition — was one of the largest churches in the Holy Land; it was built on the site of the first meeting-place of the Jerusalem Christian Community following the death of Jesus, and thus the church was known as the "Mother of All Churches". It would appear that our site is within the precincts

Two vaulted rooms, Herodian period

of that church and that various related structures stood here as well.* We have ascribed several mosaic floors to these buildings, including some uncovered long ago. A long, narrow building was cleared for 24 metres of its length, but the western part is still hidden. The adjacent street runs from north to south, towards the church. It is paved with large, well-dressed stone slabs, and heavy kerb stones, the largest of which weighs hundreds of kilogrammes. The uncovered part of the street is 44 metres long; it is 5.4. metres wide — the same width as the Byzantine street uncovered eighty years ago at the edge of Mount Zion. At the time of writing, we are tracing the continuation of this street within the walls of the Old City, and it is probable that it was one of the main streets of the city. It is further possible that it followed the course of a Herodian predecessor; if so, we could assume that it bordered the eastern limits of the Herodian palace platform (see above, p. 55).

* The Bordeaux Pilgrim (333 C.E.) already mentions that the house of the High Priest Joseph Caiaphas was located here, and the early date of this tradition concerning the site of Jesus' interrogation would tend to support its accuracy.

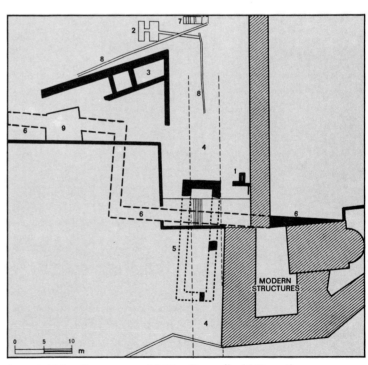

Area II. (1) Israelite structure; (2) Herodian walls; (3) Byzantine structure, used also by Crusaders; (4) Byzantine street; (5) Early Arab building; (6) Enclosure wall of Crusader monastery of St. Mary of Mount Sion; (7) Herodian cistern; (8) Byzantine water-channels; (9) Crusader cistern (originally Byzantine)

Mould for casting jewellery, 8th century C.E.

Early Arab period. At least two large structures of this period have been found in our excavations, one built in the Byzantine period, but which continued in use till Crusader times; the other was built in the Arab period and is 21 metres long. Unique finds include three moulds for casting jewellery. It is probable that in the first centuries after the Arab conquest the site remained occupied by Christian ecclesiastical bodies.

Crusader period. Immediately after the Crusader conquest of Jerusalem (see below, pp. 102 f.), the Crusaders erected a church and monastery on Mount Zion, at the site of the earlier "Church of St. Sion". This complex, which they called "St. Mary of Mount Sion", was one of the largest and wealthiest ecclesiastical institutions in the country. This church was first uncovered some 70 years ago, during the excavations for the foundations of the present Church of the Dormition. We uncovered the massive outer wall surrounding the monastery precinct, beneath which we found a large cistern, domed over. The four arches of this domed roof rest upon marble columns which had stood at the centre of the pool. The cistern was initially Byzantine, repaired by the Crusaders and used by the monastery for a hundred or so years, till destroyed apparently in 1219 C.E. The wall of the monastery continued to stand, till the monastery was finally destroyed during the raid of the Khwarismian Turks (1244 C.E.).

The "Third Wall" of Jerusalem

S. Ben-Arieh

The topography of the three walls of Jerusalem in late Second Temple times as described by Josephus (*War* VIII, 4, 2) has been the subject of a scholarly controversy for some 120 years. The course of the "Third Wall" has been especially debated; this wall, according to Josephus, was begun by Agrippa I and completed by the Zealots during the First Revolt against Rome.

In 1841, Edward Robinson first surveyed the remains of a large wall north of the walls of the modern Old City, concluding that they were part of the "Third Wall". Later in the same century, other scholars such as Conder, Schick and Merrill also expressed opinions concerning this wall. In 1925–27 and 1940, E.L. Sukenik and L.A. Mayer excavated the foundations of the wall over a course of 0.5 km, ascribing it once again to the "Third Wall". At the time, Père Vincent attacked this identification,

ascribing the wall to the days of Bar-Kokhba.

The archaeological expedition headed by Dr. Kenyon, which excavated in Jerusalem during 1961–67, also uncovered parts of the line of this wall: the work was directed by E.W. Hamrick. On the basis of their results, Dr. Kenyon concluded that the remains here represented a defensive dyke put up by the Tenth Legion during the Bar-Kokhba Revolt, while Hamrick himself ascribed them to the Zealots of the First Revolt. In the opinion of J.B. Hennessy, who excavated adjacent to Damascus Gate, the "Third Wall" followed the present line of the northern wall of the Old City.

In October 1972, excavations along the line of the "Third Wall" were renewed under the direction of Sara Ben-Arieh, E. Netzer and Y. Levi, on behalf of the Department of Antiquities and Museums and the Hebrew University of Jerusalem. It was intended

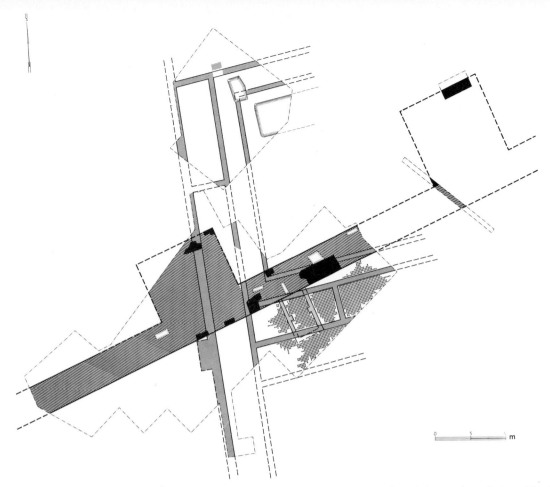

General plan of excavation area. Segment of "Third Wall", with two towers, running from left to right and pierced by Roman burials; a large Byzantine complex overlies part of the wall

to uncover a segment between Nablus Road and Hel-Hahandasa Street, and to ascertain the date of the remains.

During excavations several strata were revealed; the uppermost stratum contained a large Byzantine

Foundation of wall, looking west

Looking west along line of "Third Wall"

North-western corner of tower

building, while beneath was a row of tombs, all hewn into the base of the wall. One of these tombs had already been discovered by Sukenik and Mayer. They had been largely plundered in antiquity, and only a few objects, of the third century C.E., were found. The remains of the wall which were uncovered beneath the Byzantine level spread over a length of some 45 m and were 4.25 m wide.

The remains discovered are merely foundations, intended to level off the uneven ground and prepare it for construction of the wall proper. No attempt had been made by the builders to hew into the bedrock. The foundations were built of small field-stones as well as medium and large ashlars, bound by a limy plaster which has now hardened very much.

The surface generally slopes down toward the southeast, and thus the foundations were stepped. Technically, the segment uncovered can be divided into two parts, eastern and western. In the western part, reaching till near the edge of a tower (see below), the construction is homogeneously and continuously of field-stones. The northern and southern faces of the wall are of medium and large field-stones, while the fill between is of smaller stones, bonded with plaster. In the eastern part, ashlar construction is in more frequent use. Among the ashlars are some of 0.5–1.0 m length, one reaching 2.5 m and another even about 5 m length. The larger ashlars were laid on a base of smaller stones.

In the central part of the excavation the base of a

tower was found, jutting out some 9 m northward of the line of the wall. On the west, the tower is delimited by a wall of field-stones. At the north-eastern corner of the tower foundations, ashlar construction is found. The method of construction of these foundations is identical with that of the western part of the wall foundations — that is, with medium and large field-stones, and a fill of smaller stones between, bound with limy plaster.

In a sewage channel east of the excavation area, an ashlar was found jutting beyond the line of the wall northwards. It seems that this stone was part of a second tower, the northern wall of which is represented by another large ashlar, discovered in 1925 opposite the American Consulate.

In the eastern part of the excavation, south of the wall and beneath the Byzantine level, a broad surface of white quarry rubble came to light, apparently levelled off through treading. At one spot this surface touches upon the foundations of the wall. Above the surface, a one-room structure was found, abutting the wall. This structure may have been built up against the wall though this is not certain, for its northern and eastern parts were destroyed when the heavy foundations of the Byzantine building were laid, reaching down to bedrock. The fill of the surface contained Herodian sherds, while the fill of the room contained, besides Herodian sherds, pottery of the Byzantine period.

No building remains were discovered overlying the foundation of the wall, though a group of ashlars found in the debris nearby may indicate that the wall above was built of such stones. In any event, at several spots in the foundations, traces of large rectangular stones were discovered.

In the light of this evidence we may conclude that this was undoubtedly a continuous stretch of wall, some 75 m long, with towers jutting northward. The wall here had been about 4.30 m wide. It was erected prior to the third century C.E., when the tombs were hewn into its foundations. The early structure uncovered beneath the Byzantine building, and the surface of quarry rubble reaching the wall, indicate that the wall was built in the Herodian period — more specifically, in the first century C.E., and thus we can certainly ascribe this segment to Josephus' "Third Wall".

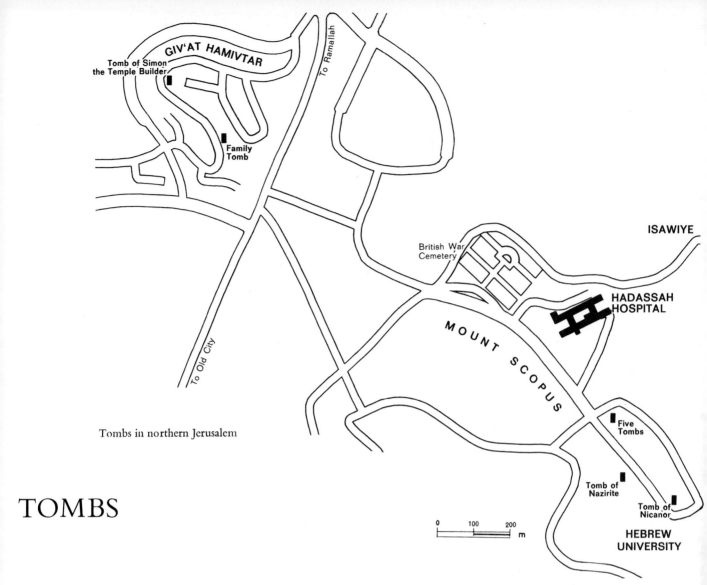

Tombs in northern Jerusalem

Map labels:
GIV'AT HAMIVTAR
Tomb of Simon the Temple Builder
Family Tomb
To Ramallah
To Old City
British War Cemetery
ISAWIYE
HADASSAH HOSPITAL
MOUNT SCOPUS
Five Tombs
Tomb of Nazirite
Tomb of Nicanor
HEBREW UNIVERSITY
0 100 200 m

TOMBS

A Recently Discovered Monolithic Tomb in Siloam

D. Ussishkin

One of the few traces of Jerusalem of the days of the Judean monarchy is the unique monumental necropolis amongst the rock cliffs on the eastern bank of the Kidron valley, in the area of Siloam village. In the Roman-Byzantine period many of the tombs were partly destroyed, and today they are to be found amongst the houses of the village. Over the last century, many of the tombs have been studied and remains of several burial-inscriptions located; only recently, however, was it possible to conduct a thorough and methodical survey and to obtain a

fuller picture of this necropolis. During the survey,* a new monumental tomb was discovered.

The most splendid and impressive of the tombs in Siloam are three monolithic tombs hewn out of the rock. Around them, too, the rock has been cut away, leaving them free-standing, and in this they resemble the famous tomb monuments of the Second Temple

* The survey was conducted by the author, assisted by G. Barkay, on behalf of the Israel Exploration Society and the Yad Ben-Zvi Memorial Foundation.

63

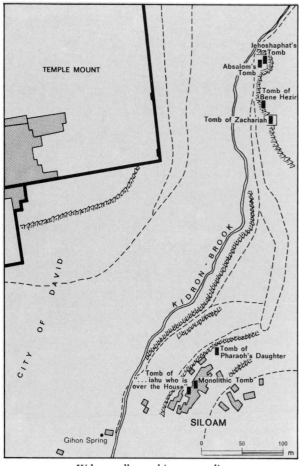

Kidron valley and its necropolis

period in Jerusalem, "Zachariah's Tomb" and "Absalom's Tomb."

The most famous of the three tombs is that known as the "Tomb of Pharaoh's Daughter". Its location, unique architecture and "Egyptian" style stirred scholarly interest already in the 19th century.

The second tomb was discovered by the Frenchman Clermont-Ganneau in 1870; he noticed two Hebrew inscriptions on the rock façade of the tomb, which he was able to purchase and ship to the

General view of Siloam village; arrow shows location of new monolithic tomb

British Museum in London. They were deciphered only a few years ago by Prof. N. Avigad: The longer inscription, which had been over the entrance to the tomb, states that it was "[the tomb of . . .]yahu, who is over the house. There is no silver and gold here but rather [his bones] and the bones of his wife (?) with him. Cursed be the man who should open this." It would appear that this was the tomb of one of the ministers of the Judean kingdom, a royal steward or chamberlain. Professors Avigad and Yadin have suggested identifying this personage with Shebna, "who is over the house", who built a splendid tomb in Jerusalem, as is known from Isaiah's invective; "What have you to do here and who have you here, that you have hewn here a tomb for yourself, you who hew a tomb on the height, and carve a habitation for yourself in the rock?" (Isaiah 22 : 16). The shorter inscription, partly defaced, has been read by Prof. Avigad as "(tomb-) chamber in the side (or slope) of the rock (or mountain) . . .", reading the last word as *hṣr*; in the present author's opinion, this last word can be restored as *hṣryh* to be interpreted as "a rock-cut chamber" and that the entire inscription relates to someone buried within the inner chamber of the tomb. Prof. Avigad has suggested that this tomb was a free-standing monolithic tomb and, indeed, our survey has confirmed this.

A third tomb is hewn into the rock north of the "Tomb of the Royal Steward." Clermont-Ganneau already noticed the dressed corner of the monolith, and a local inhabitant told him that there had been "another monument with inscriptions", now destroyed. The façade must have been covered in his day, hiding the inscription from his view. This inscription was discovered in 1940 by Prof. A. Reifenberg, and later published by him. The part of the façade bearing the inscription was relocated during our survey; and it was found to be a monolithic tomb of much finer workmanship than either of the other two. We could not expose the other sides of the monolith, for the tomb proper lies today beneath the courtyard of the house built over the adjacent "Tomb of the Royal Steward". The tomb opening in now blocked and is used as a cistern. Parts of the original opening and the roof were destroyed during Roman-Byzantine quarrying operations here.

After clearing the façade, the following details

Main street in Siloam village, with two monumental tombs; arrow on right shows location of "Royal Steward" tomb; arrow on left shows location of new monolithic tomb

and may have continued along the sides of the monolith. In the centre of the façade there is a deep niche 2.42 metres high, 1.50 metres wide and 0.50 metres deep. The relatively small opening had been cut into this niche, quite a distance above the floor of the porch. The part of the façade above the niche is smooth, and it was here that the inscription had been incised. Above this there are still traces of a projecting cornice, though the roof of the monument is entirely destroyed (possibly pyramidal, like that of the "Tomb of Pharaoh's Daughter").

The burial-inscription is clearly visible, though mostly damaged. It was of three lines and, apparently, about 74 centimetres long. Cleaning of the inscription and its reexamination enabled several minor revisions of the previous readings by Reifenberg and Avigad. Only a few words are legible in the two upper lines, but both the text and the style of the script are very similar to the inscription from the "Tomb of the Royal Steward". In the upper line, the letters of the words "burial of Z . . ." are preserved. In the second line the letters of the words "the one who op[ens . . .]" are legible, undoubtedly a warning against tampering, similar to that in the adjacent tomb. The parallel architecture and similar inscriptions would point to this also being the tomb of some high government official.

This group of monumental tombs from the period of the First Temple, like the other tombs in the Siloam necropolis, differs entirely in architectural style from the other tombs of the same period found in this country, and does not seem to represent a local style. In our opinion, we can regard this as Phoenician influence, which began making itself felt in Judah and Israel already in the time of David and Solomon.

were revealed: The monolith is 4.75 metres wide and preserved to a height of 4.25 metres. Before the façade there was a sort of hewn porch, from the centre of which a step leads up to the opening. Another step is cut along the bottom of the façade,

Photograph and facsimile of Palaeo-Hebrew inscription on façade of new monolithic tomb

The Tomb of a Nazirite on Mount Scopus

N. Avigad

On the eve of the Six Day War, when Mount Scopus was still isolated from the rest of the Jewish city, police forces stationed there, engaged in normal construction activities, happened upon an ancient burial-cave. The Department of Archaeology of the Hebrew University subsequently excavated the

Chamber in Nazirite tomb, with sarcophagi and ossuaries *in situ*

tomb. It contained four chambers: a central chamber measuring 2.45 × 2.75 metres and 2.65 metres high; and three smaller chambers (average: 1.70 × 2.20 metres). The entrance was quite small (0.60 × 0.78 metres.) The tomb had been hewn into the soft, crumbly rock, but the chamber walls and vaulting and the tomb-façade were constructed of ashlars. The workmanship was fine, of a quality rarely encountered in tombs in Jerusalem. Only the one known as "Herod's Family Tomb" resembles it in this matter. Though the entrance was sealed, the finds within had been disturbed; the ten-odd ossuaries were found scattered about, several broken and heaped up in one of the side chambers. In this latter chamber there were also two stone sarcophagi. No specific burial places had been prepared in this tomb.

Most of the ossuaries were ornamented in the common style, with rosettes, and several bear inscriptions. Two of the inscriptions are noteworthy, relating to a man and his wife: "Hanania son of Jonathan the Nazirite", and "Salome wife of Hanania son of the Nazirite". This indicates that the head of the family here was a Nazirite, that is, one under the obligation of a vow. This Jonathan may, indeed, also have been interred here, in one of the sarcophagi. The two sarcophagi are of hard limestone and their workmanship is exceedingly fine. One is plain, with a vaulted lid. The other is pleasantly ornamented with the relief of a stylized vine spreading out from the centre, with two bunches of grapes flanking. Small rosettes fill the open spaces. The gabled lid bears a rich myrtle-leaf pattern. These are common motifs in the decorative Jewish art of the period of the Second Temple. A very similar vine pattern appears on a sarcophagus found in "Herod's Family Tomb", and a similar bunch of grapes is to be seen on the façade of the Tomb of Queen Helena (the so-called "Tomb of the Kings").

Stone sarcophagus bearing floral ornamentation

The construction of the tomb is fine, the ornamentation of one of the sarcophagi is exquisite, and the inscriptions lend the tomb a special status. This seems to have been the tomb of an upper class family in Herodian times, built early in the first century C.E.

Five Jewish Burial-Caves on Mount Scopus

R. Reich and H. Geva

Within the Botanical Garden of the Hebrew University on Mount Scopus, a group of rock-hewn burial-caves was discovered in 1972; they are interconnected through breached loculi. Four of them were uncovered in their entirety, while the fifth, long-known, was collapsed and thus cleared only in part.*

The opening through which we gained access to the caves is some 70 metres northwest of the Tomb of Nicanor (see pp. 19 f.). Though the caves are connected, they do not comprise a single, intentional complex. Originally, they had been quite separate units, hewn one adjacent to the next, but during the hewing the loculi of one tomb encountered those of the next. The original openings were cleared only

on the inside, leaving the blocking stones in place. All five tombs had been plundered in antiquity.

These burial-caves are of the type common in the Second Temple period in Jerusalem. They include a squared burial chamber reached through a small doorway by descending a step or two; in the centre of this chamber is a hewn pit, leaving "benches" along three or four of the walls. Hewn into the walls are *kokhim* (loculi) — one to three (in the present case) in each wall, of a size suitable for receiving a human body.

There seems to have been a premium on burial space on Mount Scopus in the period of the Second Temple, and thus the close proximity of these tombs. This density often led the hewers to make loculi in positions quite unusual in tombs of this type, such as opening onto the pits, at a level lower than the chamber.

On the benches, in the pits and in the loculi, we

* Excavations were carried out in March 1972 on behalf of the Department of Archaeology of the Hebrew University; the find was first reported by M. Shawat, Director of the Botanical Garden, who also assisted in the excavation, as did D. Bahar.

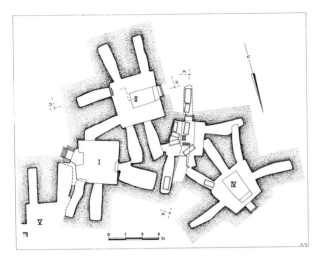

Ornamented ossuary with fluted column motif

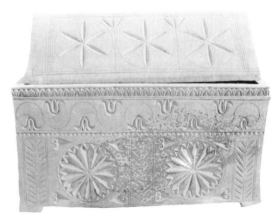

Ornamented ossuary

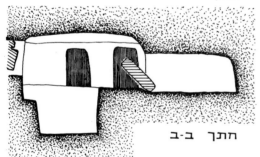

Plan and section of tomb on Mount Scopus

found a confusion of pottery, bones, earth and door-slabs (for sealing the loculi). In tomb III there were eight stone ossuaries with their lids — all of the type common in Jerusalem in late Second Temple times. Another ossuary with its lid was found in tomb IV. Several of the ossuaries were broken, and all were found open, with their lids alongside or within. Two of them were ornamented.

The front of one of the ornamented ossuaries bears, in shallow carving, the motif of a fluted column standing on a stepped base; it is flanked by large rosettes, a common motif on such ossuaries. The capital on the column seems arched and bears a wave pattern and stars; it is flanked by spirals and small leaves, in a peculiar imitation of an Ionic capital. Above the capital and in the corners of the front are branches, ivy-leaves and flowers. The other ossuary has its front divided into two horizontal panels, the lower containing two large rosettes and three vertical frames enclosing leaved branches; the rosettes are surrounded by four ivy-leaves each. In the upper panel is a wavy vine-branch with nine blossoms. The upper edge of the front bears an egg-and-dart pattern. The gabled lid bears three rosettes and schematic floral patterns. This ossuary is somewhat unusual in the ornamentation of the upper panel on the front; a similar pattern is found on stone sarcophagi, in relief (see above, p. 19). The execution and composition of the ornament here places this ossuary among the finest of the period of the Second Temple.

On one of the narrow sides of this same ossuary there is a Greek inscription, written in charcoal: IΘAPOY, "Of Itharos", most probably a Greek rendering of the Aramaic ytr', known on another ossuary.* Another inscription is carved on the gabled lid of one of the plain ossuaries: dypy EIΦEOC. This appears to be the name of the deceased in Hebrew and Greek, a name otherwise unknown on ossuaries.

* E. L. Sukenik: *Tarbiz* 6 (1935), pp. 195–196, fig. D (Hebrew).

One of the plain ossuaries is pierced on the bottom with two holes (5 mm in diameter), possibly made to allow drainage of fluids from the remains deposited within.*

Many sherds were found scattered in the tombs, all from pottery types common in the Second Temple period: cooking-pots, spindle-bottles, piriform juglets and store-jars. These date the tombs to second half of the first century B.C.E. — that is, the time of Herod the Great.

* N. Avigad: *IEJ* 21 (1971), pp. 192–194.

A Burial-Cave of the Second Temple Period at Giv'at Hamivtar

A. Kloner

During recent construction work at Giv'at Hamivtar in northern Jerusalem, several rock-hewn burial-caves of the Second Temple period have been found, containing ossuaries (see also pp. 17 ff.). One of these is a family tomb with 16 ossuaries, some bearing inscriptions*

The cave is rather carelessly hewn; there are nine loculi in the square chamber, stemming from all the walls except the front. There seem to have been several more loculi, destroyed at the time of the discovery. There is a pit in the centre of the chamber floor, with a small loculus for a secondary burial. The funerary objects, which included spindle-bottles, piriform juglets, small bowls and several cooking-pots, place the date of the tomb from the mid-first century B.C.E. to the mid-first century C.E., and possibly as late as 70 C.E. No lamps were found here, unlike in most tombs.

The cave contained the bones of thirty adults and children, though there seem to have been more deceased here, probably between 35 and 40. The remains of twenty individuals had been placed in ossuaries; those of five individuals in the central pit; and of five others in the loculi. Six of the ossuaries had been placed before loculi, and ten within loculi.

* At 52 Midbar Sinai St., excavated on behalf of the Department of Antiquities and Museums, in November 1971 and May 1972.

Investigation of the bones of twenty-one of the deceased, especially of the teeth,* revealed several interesting points: (a) At least four of the deceased were genetically related; (b) the proportion of children to adults (43:57) resembles that in other tombs of this period in Jerusalem and in antiquity in

* By Dr. Patricia Smith, of the Hebrew University-Hadassah Medical School, to whom we are most grateful.

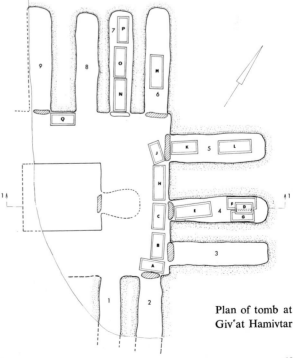

Plan of tomb at Giv'at Hamivtar

Ornamented ossuary, inscribed: "Absalom"

Inscription on rim of ossuary: *šlbydwd*

general (indeed a similar proportion is found today in "developing" countries); (c) there was no trace of nutritional deficiencies in general: (d) diets appear to have avoided sweets and protein-rich foods, but much hard food was eaten, as evidenced by the worn teeth.

Eight ossuaries were ornamented, all with a similar motif: two large rosettes within a general frame; often between the rosettes there was another element, generally floral, such as a stylized tree, a flower or leaves. Several ossuaries bear the names of the deceased; below are some of the more interesting examples.*

1. The word *qryh* may be a personal name or possibly the Greek word *kyria*, "Lady". The remains within this ossuary, however, were of three infants.

2. The names *qryh* [or *mryh*] *šm'wn*, "Kyria [or Maria] Simeon", are written in square Hebrew script, the second somewhat crudely. Several small strokes over the latter name may be intended to cancel it. This ossuary contained the remains of an adult of 40 years and of a youngster of 15.

3. The Greek word MAPEC, incised on the inner side of a lid, the ossuary of which contained the bones of a youth aged 14 and a 4-year old child.

4. The name *'bšlwm*, "Absalom", in a lapidary script. The ossuary contained the bones of a man of about 45 years.

5. The word *šlbydwd* might be interpreted as meaning "Of the sons (or house) of the uncle (cf. Bab. Tal. Yebamoth 21b), though it could as well be "Of the house of David". This ossuary, bearing a second, illegible inscription, contained the bones of a 25-year old man.

* The author wishes to thank Dr. J. Naveh and L.Y. Rahmani for their valuable comments on the inscriptions.

Ossuary (above and right), inscribed: *qryh šm'wn*

The Burial of Simon the Temple Builder

V. Tzaferis

During construction work at Giv'at Hamivtar in north-eastern Jerusalem, four Jewish tomb-caves from the end of the Second Temple period came to light. These were rectangular chambers with *kokhim* hewn into the rock walls. In three caves, ossuaries were found; the bones within them have been examined by Dr. N. Haas of the Department of Anatomy of the Hadassah-Hebrew University Medical School. One ossuary included the bones of two feet, fastened together by a nail. Dr. Haas assumes that the deceased had been crucified prior to burial.*

On about half the ossuaries there are inscriptions, deciphered by Dr. J. Naveh. One inscription is of of particular interest; it is carved twice, in two slightly different versions of spelling, on different sides of the ossuary, and reads: "Simon the Temple

* For the tomb, ossuary, bones and inscription, see *IEJ* 20 (1970), pp. 18ff.; 23 (1973), pp. 18ff.

Ossuaries as found in tomb on Giv'at Hamivtar; on right, ossuary of "Simon the Temple builder"

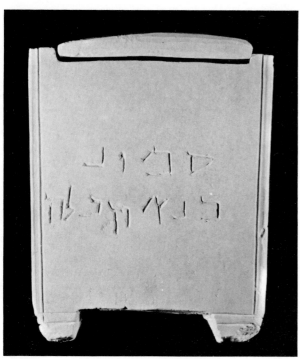

Side of ossuary, with inscription

builder". This Aramaic inscription leads us to assume that the bones in the ossuary are those of a person who took part in the construction of Herod's Temple. Since the tomb-cave is relatively modest, this Simon most likely was not *the* builder of the Temple, but rather was nicknamed (at least within his family circle) "the Temple builder". He may have been one of those responsible for work on the construction, or one of the artisans.

This inscription brings to mind the Greek inscription on an ossuary discovered in 1902 within a monumental tomb-cave on Mount Scopus, not far from Giv'at Hamivtar. It mentions "Nicanor of Alexandria who made the gates". That tomb was the burial place of a wealthy and famous family, whose head had donated the gates for Herod's Temple. The Talmudic sources often mention "the gates of Nicanor" and tell of a miracle which befell them during their voyage from Alexandria.

Façade and side of ossuary, showing inscriptions

A New Tomb-Inscription from Giv'at Hamivtar

J. Naveh

In the tomb-caves in Jerusalem from the late Second Temple period, numerous inscriptions have come to light, mostly on ossuaries, and quite short; only a very few are sufficiently long to stir especial interest. These inscriptions are written in Aramaic or Hebrew, in the "square" Jewish script, or else in Greek. Some three years ago, a relatively long Aramaic inscription came to light at Giv'at Hamivtar — written in the archaic Palaeo-Hebrew script.*

The inscription is incised in seven lines on a smoothed surface of a side tomb-chamber, above the opening to a *kokh*. In the *kokh* and within the chamber there were no objects, but in the adjacent corridor there was an ornamented ossuary. The ossuary, the plan of the tomb and its location in the midst of a large and dense Jewish cemetery all indicate that the inscription is from the late Second Temple period. It is incised within an outer frame (80 × 65 cm), with incised lines separating the lines of script. The second and fifth bands thus formed are painted reddish-brown, with the script left white; all the other incised lines and script are painted the same reddish-brown. There are no word dividers or spaces between the words. The inscription reads as follows:

'n' 'b' br khnh '/l'z(r) br 'hrn rbh 'n/h 'b' m'nyh mrd/ph dy ylyd byrwšlm / wgl' lbbl w'sq lmtt/y br hywd(h) wqbrth bm/'rth dzbnh bgth

"I, Abba, son of the priest E/leaza(r), son of Aaron the high (priest), I, / Abba, the oppressed and the persec/uted, who was born in Jerusalem, / and went into exile in Babylonia and brought (back [to Jerusalem]) Mattath/iah son of Juda(h), and I buried him in the c/ave, which I acquired by the writ."

This is a most unusual inscription in its form, content and script, and its author has attempted to give it a monumental character. Further, it gives relatively much information on the "benefactor", Abba, but little on the deceased, Mattathiah. It is also surprising that it is written in the Palaeo-Hebrew script, in spite of the language being Aramaic.

In the period of the Second Temple there was a decided decline in the use of the old Hebrew script, which had developed in First Temple times as the Israelite national script. Aramaic and its script came to replace Hebrew and the archaic script almost entirely. The older script was still used in some Hebrew inscriptions and manuscripts, such as coins and some scrolls of the Bible, but the Judeo-Aramaic script was dominant, even in sacred texts. Most of the Bible manuscripts found at Qumran near the Dead Sea, though Hebrew in language, are written in this Aramaic script. The archaic writing and the Hebrew language were employed by the Hasmonean kings and the leaders of the two revolts against Rome, and Pentateuch fragments have been found at Qumran written entirely in this script, or with the Tetragrammaton so written. And recently part of a monumental inscription in the archaic script came to light in the excavations adjacent to the Temple Mount (see above, p. 35). All these seem to be instances in which nationalistic motives dictated the choice of script.

The Samaritans also use a form of the early Hebrew script, to the present day. It is their sole script for their texts and over the years they have used it for writing Hebrew, Aramaic and even Arabic — for both sacred and profane matters. The earliest known inscriptions specifically in the Samaritan script are from the third century C.E.

* The inscription was discovered by A. and D. Rosenthal and A. Spitzer, who notified the Department of Antiquities and Museums. Prof. E. S. Rosenthal first deciphered and published the text.

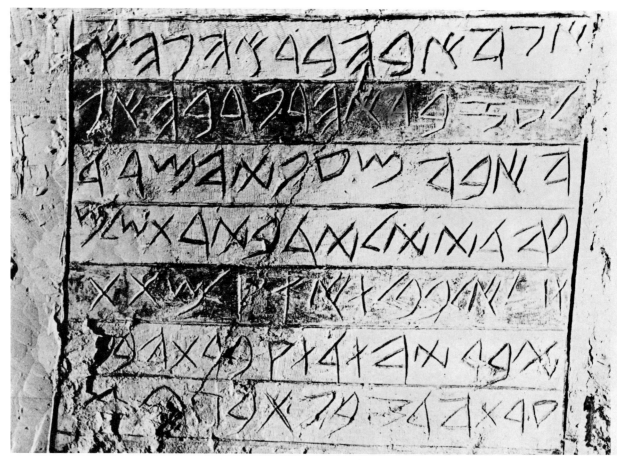

Tomb inscription at Giv'at Hamivtar

The latest appearance of the archaic Hebrew script among the Jews was during the Bar Kokhba Revolt, in the second century C.E.

From the above, it might be concluded that our inscription is Samaritan and, indeed, several of the letter-forms are quite close to the Samaritan forms. The opening formula also resembles that found in certain Samaritan documents. However, the priestly line noted in the inscription appears to be Jewish, and the names Mattathiah and Judah are definitely Jewish in character and were very common in Hasmonean times. Further, the fact that the inscription was found in Jerusalem, and that the author was born in this city, are decisive in ascribing it to a Jewish family.

But why was the inscription written in the Palaeo-Hebrew script? The use of this script was a source of controversy in Talmudic times, and apparently even earlier, there having been sectarian differences on this matter. The Pharisees, whose views are reflected in the Talmud, preferred the "square" Aramaic script, but it appears that other sects did use the archaic form. We cannot at present know whether these were the Essenes or the Sadducees, or some other unknown faction. In any event, we may confidently assume that the inscription before us was not Pharisaic.

This may serve to explain the unusual character of the inscription, as far as script and content are concerned. But we are still left with several open questions: Why was Abba persecuted and by whom? Was his exile self-imposed, or was he exiled to Babylonia, and by whom? Who was Mattathiah, to whom Abba was sufficiently devoted to transport his remains to Jerusalem for burial? Unfortunately, we must remain in the dark on all these points.

WATER SUPPLY

The Water Supply of Israelite Jerusalem

R. Amiran

The only spring* in the immediate vicinity of Jerusalem is En-Gihon, which flows forth in the Kidron bed, at the foot of the south-eastern spur of the city. The spring led to the founding of the earliest settlement of Jerusalem, on the ridge known in ancient times as Zion or Mount Zion. This Gihon spring served as the sole source of water for the population of Jerusalem for many generations, till means were devised to divert rainfall to open reservoirs and rock-hewn cisterns. It can be assumed that this development, which apparently came in the Middle Bronze Age II, freed the city from absolute dependence upon the natural supply. The water supply for the Temple and palace built by King Solomon on the north-eastern hill — the Temple Mount — was evidently based upon rock-hewn cisterns. We can also assume that the expansion of the city, into such areas as the "Mishne" and the western hill — which began during the Judean monarchy and continued in Hasmonean and Herodian times (8th-1st centuries B.C.E.) — relied upon diverted and stored water, whether in large, open pools or in cisterns. In the days of Herod, new heights were reached when waters were diverted and brought from sources far away from Jerusalem.

The Gihon is a typical karst spring, and its waters gush intermittently (this may be the origin of the Hebrew name: *giha*, "a gushing forth"). Each gush lasts about 40 minutes, with a break of about 6–8 hours between, according to season. The discharge is about 1200 cubic metres per day, though in summer it drops considerably. All through history, the spring's waters served for drinking and for irrigating the city's gardens. In all periods, the spring

was located outside the city-walls (as recently proved by Kathleen Kenyon); there must have been a gate close to the spring, the "Water Gate" (e. g. Nehemiah 8 : 3, 16). Père H. Vincent studied the spring and the related water installations in 1908–1911 and described them in detail.* Much later, M. Hecker reviewed and summarized the general subject of water supply to Jerusalem.**

* Père L. H. Vincent: *Jerusalem sous terre*, London, 1911.
** In M. Avi-Yonah, ed.: *Sepher Yerushalayim* I, Jerusalem, 1956 (Hebrew).

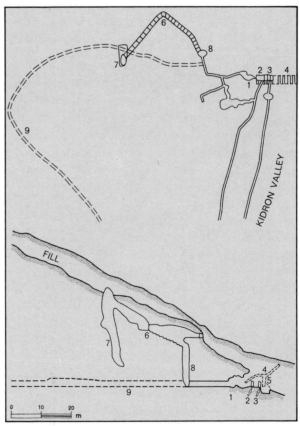

* En-Rogel, some 150 metres south of the confluence of the Kidron and Hinnom valleys, is apparently a well. The position of the En-Gihon spring of today shows that the wadi-bed has risen here almost 12 metres and shifted westward over the last three millennia.

En-Gihon and Warren's Shaft. (1) Spring; (2–3) damming walls; (4) stairway down to water-level; (5) natural cave; (6) Jebusite tunnel; (7) upper shaft; (8) lower shaft; (9) Hezekiah's Tunnel

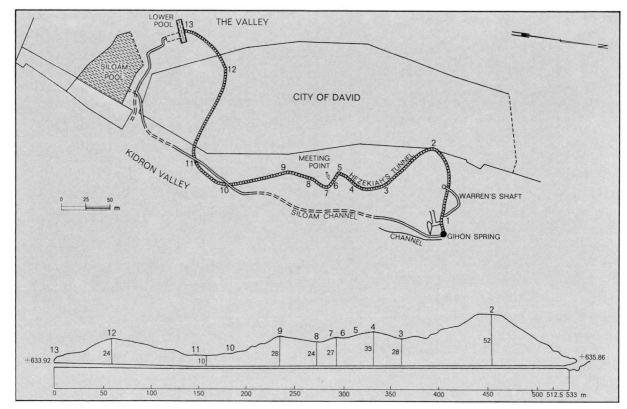

En-Gihon, Siloam channel and Hezekiah's Tunnel

Two early water projects in Jerusalem — "Warren's Shaft"* and Hezekiah's Tunnel — were constructed according to principles found also at other ancient Canaanite and Israelite cities in this country. The main incentive behind this was undoubtedly defensive — the need for secure access to the water source, concealed from the eyes of the enemy, as well as preventing him from utilizing it himself (cf., e.g., 2 Chronicles 32 : 4: "Why should the kings of Assyria come, and find much water?").

The date of Warren's Shaft is difficult to determine; in contrast, Hezekiah's Tunnel is well documented in the Bible, and is commemorated also in the famous inscription found at its lower end. The latter tunnel was hewn ca. 701 B.C.E. Warren's Shaft must be dated entirely on the basis of analogy and historical logic. This eliminates the possibility of the shaft being later than Hezekiah's Tunnel; moreover, it would seem that it was old and long disused already in Hezekiah's time. Unfortunately, analogy does not come to our aid to any sufficient

degree in dating Warren's Shaft. The water tunnel at Megiddo can now be dated to the days of Ahab (rather than the Late Bronze Age), and the one at Gibeon, to sometime in the period of the Judean Monarchy.* We cannot deal here with the two principal types of subterranean tunnels and their development from the chronological aspect; this could lead, again, only to a very general dating of the shaft. The technique of work is also of little aid.

Warren's Shaft is a tunnel entered from above the spring, about half-way up the slope in what must have been a region of public buildings within the ancient city-walls. The shaft comprises three elements: a stepped tunnel, hewn into the rock, 39 metres long and descending 12.7 metres deep; a vertical shaft some 11 metres deep; and a horizontal channel 20 metres long, leading the spring waters into the interior of the hill, to the base of the vertical shaft. Water was drawn from the horizontal channel up the vertical shaft by means of buckets, and thence carried up the stepped tunnel.

* This shaft is named after Charles Warren, who discovered it in 1867.

* Cf. Y. Yadin: *IEJ* 8 (1958), pp. 80–86: J. Pritchard: *The Water System of Gibeon*, Philadelphia, 1961.

Hezekiah's Tunnel is properly considered to be the largest of the known ancient hydro-technical projects in this country. Besides its military aspect, it reflects true town-planning (cf. " . . . and brought water into the city . . . " [2 Kings 20: 20], which can be interpreted as meaning that the exit was located within the city-walls of Hezekiah's time). Further, this project enabled the full exploitation of the flow of the spring by channeling the waters to a single large reservoir, providing absolute control over the water. The curved tunnel is 533 metres long, though the straight-line distance is only 320 metres. Its slope is very gentle, some 2.18 metres (0.4%). The height of the tunnel varies between 1.1 and 3.4 metres. The evidence in the Bible and the finely carved inscription relating the meeting of the two teams hewing the tunnel (see below) complement one another.

The Bible relates of Hezekiah's Tunnel:

2 Kings 20:20: "And the rest of the acts of Hezekiah, and his might, and how he made a pool, and a conduit, and brought water into the city, are they not written in the book of the chronicles of the kings of Judah?"

Isaiah 22:11: "Ye made also a channel between the two walls for the water of the old pool."

2 Chronicles 32:2-4: "And when Hezekiah saw that Sennacherib was come, and that he was purposed to fight against Jerusalem, he took counsel with his princes and his mighty men to stop the waters of the fountains which were without the city and they did help him. So there was gathered much people together, who stopped all the fountains, and the brook that ran through the midst of the land, saying, Why should the kings of Assyria come, and find much water?"

2 Chronicles 32:30: "This same Hezekiah also stopped the upper watercourse of Gihon, and brought it straight down to the west side of the city of David. And Hezekiah prospered in all his works."

Ben Sira 48:17: "Hezekiah fortified his city, and brought in water into the midst thereof: he digged the hard rock with iron, and made wells for waters."

The broad S-curve of the tunnel, and the manner of the meeting of the two teams, have been the subject of a considerable literature, and the various theories can be divided into two groups: (1) that

Hezekiah's Tunnel

of Clermont-Ganneau,* who believed the curved course of the tunnel to be due to the desire to avoid the "Tombs of the Davidic Kings" in the City of David; and (2) that of Hecker,** who believes that the engineers and hewers followed a stratum in the rock which was of a medium hardness, known as *meleke*. It seems to me, however, that the major difficulty of the undertaking was not the actual hewing with the primitive iron tools of that day, but rather the problem of ventilation within so long a tunnel, even if worked from both ends simultaneously. A suggestion was made long ago by Sulley*** that the curved course of the tunnel indicates the former existence of a natural subterranean stream which ran from the spring through the hill, emerging at the bottom of the valley on the west of the Mount Zion spur. The problem of the ventilation can be answered by a flow of air which would natually have been associated with it.

Many points which have been enigmatic till now can be clarified in the light of this last theory: (a) The engineers could plan their work from both sides and be sure of success, for the two ends of the

* For a summary of his view, see J. Simons: *Jerusalem in the Old Testament*, Leiden, 1952, pp. 212ff.
** M. Hecker, in *Sepher Yerushalayim* I, pp. 195–197 (Hebrew).
*** H. Sulley: *PEFQSt* 1929, p. 124.

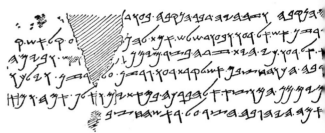

Siloam Inscription, from Hezekiah's Tunnel (photograph and facsimile)

stream already were known to meet, and all the hewers had to do was to follow them. (2) The biblical "brook that ran through the midst of the land" (2 Chronicles 32:4) can now be interpreted properly, precisely defining this natural underground stream. (3) The word *zdh* in the third line of the inscription, the etymology of which remains obscure, can now be explained as a technical term for a crack in the rock through which water and air could pass. In this same line, "on the right and [on the left]" seems to refer to the relationship of the respective teams of hewers to the stream, coming from opposite sides. (4) Reference to the "Upper Gihon" in the Bible would indicate that the spot where the underground stream emerged, in the area which later became the lower pool, was known as the "Lower Gihon". (5) All these suggestions lead to the assumption that the ancients knew that the waters of the Upper Gihon were connected with those of the Lower Gihon, and actually formed a single "stream". In this, they were undoubtedly aided by the specific gushing character of this source.

The Siloam Tunnel Inscription

"...the tunnelling (was finished). And this was the matter of the tunnelling: While [the hewers wielded] the axe, each man toward his fellow, and while there were still three cubits to be he[wn, there was hear]d a man's voice call/ing to his fellow, for there was a crack (?) in the rock on the right and [on the lef]t. And at the end of the/tunnelling the hewers hacked each man towards his fellow, axe upon axe. And there flowed / the waters from the spring towards the reservoir for two hundre[d and] a / thousand cubits. And a hu[nd]red cubits was the height of the rock above the head(s) of the hewers."

The Aqueducts of Jerusalem

A. Mazar

The great expansion of Jerusalem in the days of the Second Temple raised a serious problem of water supply. The local sources — the Gihon spring, cisterns and reservoirs — were no longer sufficient, especially during the three annual pilgrimages. The problem here was overcome — as in many cities in the Hellenistic-Roman world — by constructing a series of aqueducts to bring water from afar. The Talmud several times mentions an aqueduct in connection with the Temple: "An aqueduct led to it from Etam" (Pal. Tal. Yoma 41a); "The spring of Etam is higher than the floor of the court [of the Temple] (by) twenty-three cubits" (Bab. Tal. Yoma 31a); the Talmud further relates that the waters of the aqueduct were used for ritual immersion by the High Priest (Bab. Tal. Zebahim 54b). Josephus relates of riots in Jerusalem in the days of Pontius Pilate, caused by the Procurator's use of Temple funds for the construction of a new aqueduct for the city. The destruction of this same aqueduct

The Arrub aqueduct crossing cliff-face (point 11 in map, p. 83)

Barrel-vaulting over Wadi Biyar aqueduct (point 23)

by the Sicarii during the First Revolt seems to be indicated by another source: "The aqueduct which used to come from Etam, Sicarii once came and destroyed it" (Lamentations Rabba 4 : 4). This spring at Etam is identified with 'Ain 'Atan just below Solomon's Pools. Already in the 19th century, Charles Wilson located the aqueduct from this spring to Jerusalem; he identified two aqueducts bringing water from Solomon's Pools to Jerusalem — the Lower Aqueduct, from 'Ain 'Atan to the Temple Mount, and the Upper Aqueduct, some 30 metres higher. Conrad Schick, who systematically studied the network of aqueducts here, discovered two more, leading to Solomon's Pools from springs concentrated in Wadi Arrub and Wadi Biyar. Since the publication of Schick's work, in 1878, no systematic survey of the aqueducts had been carried out. Upon the establishment of a Field School at Kfar 'Esion, Y. Kohen, its founder, initiated such a survey,* encompassing an examin-

* The survey was carried out in 1969 by the author and Y. Cohen (assisted by a staff from the Field School) on behalf of the Israel Academy of Sciences and Humanities, under the supervision of Prof. M. Even-Ari, Ruth Amiran and L. Shenan. For an earlier summary of the subject of the ancient water supply in Jerusalem, see M. Hecker, in *Sepher Yerushalayim* I, pp. 213–218 (and the bibliography there, on p. 427) (Hebrew).

ation of the sources tapped by the aqueducts, mapping of the aqueducts and description of their visible remains. In addition, the literary sources shedding light on the history of the aqueducts from their construction to the present day have been gathered.

The flow of water to Jerusalem, as in all Roman aqueducts, was solely by gravity, Thus, the sources had to be higher than the city being supplied. Such sources are found south of Jerusalem in three concentrations: in Wadi Arrub, where the springs are an average of 810 metres above sea-level; in Wadi Biyar, at the southern end of which there is a spring at the 870 metre level; and in the region of Solomon's Pools, where there are two springs above the pools, at 800 metres, and two more below the pools, at the 765 metre level. The final destination of the Lower Aqueduct — the Temple Mount — lies at the 735 metre level. These very slight differences in height, and the numerous topographical obstructions, necessitated a meandering, lengthy route for the aqueducts, with a very slight gradient.

The first section of the aqueduct system, which we call the Arrub Aqueduct, runs from 'Ain Kuweiziba on the south (1, on the map) to the middle of Solomon's Pools. This region is split up by a number of small wadis, necessitating a route of some 40 kilometres, even though the distance is only 10 kilometres as the crow flies. The aqueduct gathers the abundant waters of the springs of Wadi Arrub, partly stored in a pool of some 20,000 cubit metres capacity (4). In this region, the aqueduct is built on a high foundation wall, but in the rocky region east of Beit Fajjar it is a mere channel hewn into the bedrock, or partly hewn and partly constructed, covered over by stone slabs. In this section, it is some 50 centimetres wide and 50–60 centimetres high. In three places (8–9 and 14) the aqueduct tunnels beneath ridges; the bridging of wadis was done by means of solid dams which could withstand the winter torrents. All along the Arrub Aqueduct, two major building phases can be distinguished. The initial stage is probably to be ascribed to the period of the Second Temple; whereas the second stage is apparently from Mamluk times. This can be gathered from an account by the German pilgrim Felix Faber, who visited this country in 1480–1483; after describing Solomon's Pools and the aqueduct to Jerusalem (the lower one), he relates: "Above these pools, on the opposite side of the mountains, we saw more than six hundred infidels digging and working to bring new waters to the old ones in Jerusalem; for water has been found . . . a long way off . . . The Sultan [Qaitbai] is striving to bring into Jerusalem . . . with vast toil . . . leading a watercourse through the hollows of many mountains, through cuttings in the rock and clearances of stones, for a distance of eight German miles, down a slope made by measurements in due proportion. Moreover, he is renewing the old watercourses, is making many tanks for the storage of rain-water . . ." (Palestine Pilgrims' Text Society, *Felix Fabri* II, p. 200).

The aqueduct of Wadi Biyar is a short one, with a fairly straight route, mostly through tunnels. It is some 4.7 kilometres long and differs entirely from the Arrub Aqueduct. The first three kilometres of the Biyar Aqueduct — from the spring ('Ain el-Daraj) to point 23 on the map — is actually one long tunnel, hewn at a depth of 8–23 metres along the wadi. The tunnel was hewn through tens of shafts, a well-known technique employed in Roman aqueducts. Tunnels of this type were generally employed to overcome topographical obstacles, but here the intent differed; the wadi provided no obstacle, especially since the opening of the tunnel is some 70 metres above the upper reservoir at Solomon's Pools. The intent here for hewing the tunnel was purely hydraulic, showing the knowledge of the engineers involved. The tunnel is hewn into soft *ḥawwar*, an impermeable limestone giving rise to springs throughout the Judean hills. The geologist A. Flexer, who has examined the tunnel, writes: "The principle of building the tunnel is in the meeting of an aquifer and an aquiclud, so that all along the way ground water is constantly being gathered." Thus, we have before us a unique hydraulic project, having no parallel in this country; the entire tunnel was hewn to serve as a water-source — three kilometres long! This is the well-known system of the *qanat* (or *fuqqar*) in Persia, which the Romans copied throughout their empire. The extreme difference between this aqueduct and that of Wadi Arrub is emphasized by the fact that in the continuation farther north it passes through another tunnel, 400 metres long (24), whereas the Arrub Aqueduct makes a circuit around the same hill in an exposed channel (16–17), only a short distance away. The efficiency of the Biyar Aqueduct is indicated by the fact that, after the British conquest

Lower aqueduct, tunnel near Government House (point 22)

of Palestine, when the water supply to Jerusalem was again a major problem, the Mandatory authorities refurbished Solomon's Pools and rebuilt the Biyar Aqueduct, which is still in use today as the prime source for filling the Pools.

Above Solomon's Pools there are two springs: 'Ain Saleh and 'Ain Burak. These springs possess various installations intended to capture a maximum of their yield: These include hewn ducts, barrel-vaulted chambers and subterranean aqueducts leading the waters to the Pools and to the Lower Aqueduct. Similar installations are found at 'Ain Farruji, below the lower Pool. They seem to have been built in the period of the Second Temple, like other similar installations in the Judean hills.

The waters from Solomon's Pools and the springs surrounding them are led to the Temple Mount in the Lower Aqueduct, 21 kilometres long. This aqueduct was built already in Second Temple

Section of upper aqueduct, near Rachel's Tomb

times, though many modifications have been made since then. In only a few places are there original sections (18, 20 and 22), most of the visible remains being, apparently, from Mamluk times. In the Ottoman period a ceramic pipe was laid in the plastered channel, made of fitted segments; it was not very efficient and often became clogged. The Lower Aqueduct tunnelled through two ridges; the

Single segment of aqueduct pictured above

first tunnel, today blocked, passed beneath the town of Bethlehem and was some 400 metres long. The second tunnel, which is still well preserved, passed through the Jebel Mukabbir ridge west of Government House (22); it is 370 metres long, with only a few access shafts. Already in the 19th century Warren and Bliss discovered two lines of the aqueducts on the southern slope of Mount Zion; the earlier one is hewn into the rock, while the Mamluk-Ottoman one is a channel running between two stone walls, covered over with stone slabs. Further sections of both these can be seen on the eastern slope of the Jewish Quarter, within the Old City, at the stairs leading from the Jewish Quarter to the Western Wall plaza. The aqueduct ran on to the Temple Mount over "Wilson's Arch", coming to an end in the huge cistern system there. We have no data on the precise date of its construction. Its important role for the Temple rites negates its equation with the aqueduct built by Pilate with Temple funds. More reasonable is the assumption that the aqueduct from 'Ain 'Atan was already in existence in the days of Herod and was possibly built even under the Hasmoneans. Pilate's aqueduct can possibly be identified with the Arrub Aqueduct.

The Upper Aqueduct leaves the upper of Solomon's Pools at the 790 metre level, and runs to

Jerusalem aqueduct system. Legend: 1 — Turkish channel;
2 — Roman channel; 3 — Second Temple period channels;
4 — tunnel

Arrub aqueduct: (1) Barrel-vault over spring; (2) segment hewn
into rock; (3) crossing of brook (two building phases evident);
(4) Arrub pool; (5–6) crossing of brook on dam 4.5 m thick;
(7) crossing of brook on dam 23 m long; (8, 9) tunnels through
ridges; (10) square guard fort; (11) channel hewn 2.5 m into
rock for 25 m; (12) crossing of brook on bridge; (13) cutting
through ridge; (14) tunnel through ridge, 156 m long; (15) crossing cliff-face in channel 2.5 m deep; (16) crossing Wadi Artas
on dam; (17) hewn channel and short tunnel crossing cliff-face

Lower aqueduct: (18) segment of old aqueduct hewn in rock;
(19) hewn channel, from old aqueduct; (20) channel and short
tunnel, from old aqueduct; (21) cisterns and agricultural installations along aqueduct; (22) opening of tunnel on Jebel Mukabbir

Biyar aqueduct: (23) end of Wadi Biyar tunnel; ancient pool and
modern dam; (24) tunnel

Upper aqueduct: (25) hewn and constructed segments on rocky
slope; (26) pipe built of huge stone segments; (27–28) hewn
sections; (19) constructed section

Herodian aqueduct: (30) hewn sections; (31) hewn and constructed
sections; (32) crossing of brook; (33) hewn and plastered sections
in soft limestone

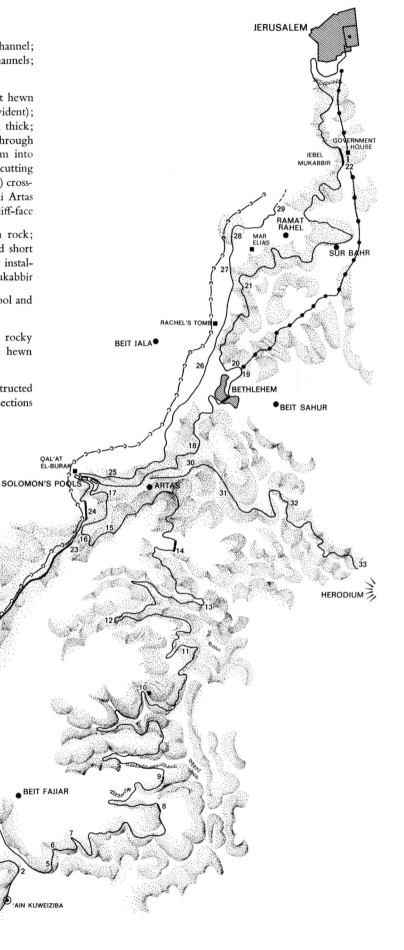

Lower aqueduct, uncovered near Abu-Tor, south of Old City

Jerusalem along a line almost exactly corresponding with the water-divide, that is, the Bethlehem-Jerusalem road. In a survey along this aqueduct, sections were found hewn into the rock or built of field stones and plaster — up to a point north of Mar Elias monastery (29). In the low part of the valley near Rachel's Tomb (26), the aqueduct passed through a huge pipe of well-made stone segments, carefully fitted; this pipe is some 2.5 kilometres long, but is preserved for only short stretches. In the past, segments of this pipe have been found bearing inscriptions of commanders of the Tenth Legion; the Upper Aqueduct was built to supply water for this legion's camp in the area of today's Citadel, at a level of about 765 metres above sea-level. A hewn tunnel of this Upper Aqueduct was discovered

quite recently, to the west of the Yemin Moshe quarter in Jerusalem, at a level slightly higher than the Citadel; this seems to have carried water to the largest cistern in Jerusalem — Hezekiah's Pool.

The network of aqueducts around Jerusalem is clear evidence of the continual efforts to maintain a regular water supply for the city. The many literary sources and remains *in situ* indicate that this network grew gradually, but at least the oldest part — the Lower Aqueduct — was in continuous use for a very lengthy period. Only some 70 years ago, the Ottoman authorities refurbished parts of the Lower Aqueduct, and it was only under the British Mandate, after the modern pump-houses had been installed, that iron pipes were laid, putting the aqueduct out of commission finally.

The Location of the Seleucid Akra in Jerusalem

Y. Tsafrir

The building of the Akra in 168 B.C.E. was possibly the principal step taken by Antiochus IV Epiphanes to secure his rule and the position of the Hellenizers in Jerusalem. Josephus describes this fortress as follows: "… after he had overthrown the city walls, he built the Akra (citadel) in the Lower City, for the place was high, and overlooked the temple; on which account he fortified it with high walls and towers, and put into it a garrison of Macedonians. Moreover, in that citadel dwelt the impious and wicked part of the [Jewish] multitude, from whom it proved that the citizens suffered many and sore calamities" (*Antiquities* XII, 252). Until it was razed by Simeon Maccabeus in 141 B.C.E., this fortress was the stronghold and symbol of Greco-Syrian rule in Jerusalem. Towering high above the Temple, it was the object of military attacks and political pressures, and according to the Book of Maccabees and Ta'anit, its downfall was celebrated as a holiday.

Over the years, the precise site of the Akra was forgotten and in modern research it has become one of the most controversial facets of ancient Jerusalem. The various theories and suggestions can generally be divided into two major groups. Some scholars — including G.A. Smith, Schürer and Simons — follow Josephus' placing the Akra in the Lower City, that is, on the south-eastern hill of Jerusalem. Others — including Robinson, Warren, Vincent, and Avi-Yonah — prefer to locate it in the Upper City, even if this negates Josephus, regarding it as the more suitable site, overlooking the Temple across the Tyropoeon valley; that area, too, would have been more suitable for the construction of a Hellenistic city. This view has generally been accepted, even after Tcherikover proved that the foundation of the *polis* of Antiochia in Jerusalem (1 Maccabees 4:9) did not refer to the building of a new city or even quarter, but only that the city received a new status, that of Hellenistic *polis*. Generally, this theory placed

the Akra itself somewhere in the area of the modern Jewish Quarter. That there were no major Hellenistic buildings in this area, however, is now being revealed by the current excavations there (see above, pp. 41 ff.); the pottery from prior to the first century B.C.E. is quite sparce and appears only in fills. On the other hand, some Hellenistic pottery and coins have been found in Prof. B. Mazar's excavations (see above, pp. 25 ff.) south and west of the Temple Mount; this early Hellenistic assemblage supplements the finds from other excavations in the Lower City, especially the rich, well-dated material discovered by Crowfoot on the western slope of the City of David.

The above considerations would appear to shed doubt upon the likelihood of locating the Akra on the west and to accept the suggestion of locating it on the south-eastern hill. Moreover, it further appears that in the period preceding the Hasmoneans

"Seam" near south-eastern corner of Temple Mount

the city apparently included only the area of the Lower City and its slopes, and the Temple Mount. The latter and the adjacent fortress formed the city's acropolis. Already at the end of the 19th century, Schürer discerned a double usage of the term "Akra": At first it was a Ptolemaic fortress, apparently erected north of the Temple — as mentioned in the account of the conquest of Jerusalem by Antiochus III in 200 B.C.E. (*Antiquities* XII, 133, 138). From the days of Antiochus IV on, the name referred to a huge fortress which, as Josephus claims, was built south of the Temple Mount (*War* I, 39; *Antiquities* XII, 252).

The different positioning of the two Akra fortresses stems from different problems motivating their construction. The Ptolemaic fortress (which most probably stood on the site of one of the towers of Nehemiah's time) defended the topographically weak spot north of the Temple (the same factor later led the Hasmoneans to build the "Baris" fortress on this flank). In contrast, Antiochus IV built his Akra for the internal struggle over control within the city; this was the citadel of the Hellenizers, and it was intended to control the Temple and the pagan cult instituted by them. Thus it was built within the city, south of the Temple. Functionally the Seleucid Akra resembled the Antonia fortress built by Herod and utilized by the Romans (see below, pp. 87 ff.). There may have been some sort of rise, or a cliff, here, south of the Temple, but we can assume that the raising of the Akra above the level of the Temple was by means of a built platform.

The suggestion below depicts the Seleucid Akra southeast of the Temple, in an area today covered by the Herodian Temple Mount. Our discussion is largely theoretical, for we know nothing of the structures of this period in this region. We can assume that the area south of the Temple was then cut through by a street ascending from the Lower City to the Temple along the ridge. In selecting a site east of this street, the Seleucids could control not only the approach but also the forecourt of the Temple, to its east, where the multitude would gather. This location would better explain the motives behind the fierce struggle and hatred felt by the Jews for the Akra. It would also make various passages and descriptions in the Book of Maccabees and in Josephus better understood: How the Akra garrison and Hellenizing refugees in the Akra could sortie out and slaughter Jews coming to sacrifice at the Temple (*Antiquities* XII, 362); how Judas Maccabeus could order some of his troops to divert the attention of the Akra guards while he himself carried out the purification of the Temple (*War* I, 39; *Antiquities* XII, 318; 1 Maccabees 4:41); how Nicanor could descend from the Akra to the Temple (*Antiquities* XII, 406).

Southeast of the Temple lies an early stretch of masonry in the Eastern Wall of the Temple Mount, north of the "seam" there. This "seam", some 32 metres north of the southeastern corner of the Temple Mount, is the joint of the huge masonry of Herod's project with the corner of an earlier structure. The fact that the Herodian courses are fitted to the older ones proves their chronological relationship. The "seam" itself was noted by Warren already in 1870, but only in 1965 did the Jordanian Department of Antiquities expose a part of the older masonry here, to a depth of seven courses. This masonry has been identified by Durand with the wall of the Temple Mount built by Zerubbabel toward the end of the 6th century B.C.E. and, alternatively, ascribed to the Hellenistic period. Another proposal is that this early corner was the corner of the Temple Mount in Hasmonean times. It is at present difficult to ascertain how far north this early masonry reaches; Warren was able to trace it for only some 17 metres. The masonry resembles that of the Herodian courses, but the ashlars are not as long. The stone-dressing is precise, with narrow, smooth margins leaving a flat but projecting boss; somewhat resembling that of constructions at other sites generally ascribed to the Hasmonean period. In the present instance, the workmanship is much finer, though not as fine as the Herodian masonry, adjacent. The closest parallel is the masonry of the Hellenistic fortifications in Greece and Asia Minor.

In a future, detailed study, we hope to prove the Seleucid date of this earlier masonry; this would make it tempting to identify these Hellenistic remains within the Eastern Wall of the Temple Mount with the foundations of the Seleucid Akra. Lacking any tangible data, however, this must remain entirely hypothetical.

The Archaeological Reconstruction of the Antonia Fortress

P. Benoit, O.P.

It is generally agreed that a fortress was located adjacent to the north-western corner of the Temple Mount; this fortress was rebuilt by Herod and named "Antonia" after Mark Anthony. It is thus clear that it was constructed prior to the battle of Actium (31 B.C.E.). Josephus describes this structure as follows: "Now as to the tower of Antonia, it was situated at the corner of two cloisters of the court of the Temple; of that on the west, and that on the north; it was erected upon a rock of fifty cubits in height, and was on a great precipice ... In the first place, the rock itself was covered over with smooth pieces of stone, from its foundation, both for ornament and that anyone who would either try to get up or to go down it might not be able to hold his feet upon it. Next to this, and before you come to the edifice of the tower itself, there was a wall of three cubits height; but within that wall all the space of the tower of Antonia itself was built upon, to the height of forty cubits. The inward parts had the largeness and form of a palace, it being parted into all kinds of rooms and other conveniences, such as courts, and places for bathing, and broad spaces for camps...And as the entire structure resembled that of a tower, it contained also four other distinct towers at its four corners; whereof the others were but fifty cubits high; whereas that which lay upon the southeast corner was seventy cubits high, that from thence the whole temple might be viewed; but on the corner where it joined to the two cloisters of the temple, it had passages down to them both, through which the guard ... went several ways among the cloisters, with their arms, on the Jewish festivals, in order to watch the people, that they might not there attempt to make any innovations; for the Temple was a fortress that guarded the city, as was the tower of Antonia a guard to the temple; and in that tower were the guards of those three" (*War* V, 238–245).

There are two main problems concerning this fortress, one archaeological and the other historical:[*] (a) How was the fortress built and precisely what area did it occupy? (b) Is the Antonia fortress identical with the Roman praetorium mentioned in the Gospels as the place where Pilate condemned Jesus?

The author's view concerning the second point, which is now generally accepted, is that the praetorium, that is, the Roman administrative centre, was located in Herod's palace on the western side of the city. Josephus and Philo both testify that the Roman governors stayed there while in Jerusalem, and the Gospels' description would suit this site better than any other.

Students of the topography of Jerusalem have been concerned with the problem of the location and structure of the Antonia fortress for many years, and excavations have been carried out on the assumed site. The conflicting conclusions of the excavators are reflected in the various reconstructions which have been proposed, whether in drawings or in models,[**] the most famous of which is that at the "Holyland" Hotel in Jerusalem, recreating Jerusalem of the Second Temple period.

Perusal of the ancient sources dealing with the Antonia fortress, and careful study of the site itself, have led the author to conclude that none of the reconstructions of this building are correct. This is especially evident in three points:

(A) **The pavement** of the courtyard is generally regarded as being from the time of Herod. It is thought to be the inner court of the fortress, commonly identified with the *Lithostrotos*, the stone

---

[*] See P. Benoit: *Revue biblique* 59 (1952), pp. 531–550.

[**] See L.H. Vincent: *Revue biblique* 42 (1933), pp. 83–113; 59 (1952), pp. 513–350; 61 (1954), pp. 87–107; idem, *Jérusalem de l'Ancien Testament* I, Paris, 1954, pp. 193–221; Soeur Marie-Aline: *La forteresse Antonia à Jérusalem et la question du Prétoire*, Jerusalem. 1956.

Model of "Antonia Fortress" at Holyland Hotel

pavement where Pilate condemned Jesus. This pavement, however, had no connection with either Jesus or the Antonia fortress; it is merely a Roman forum from the days of Hadrian.

It is most difficult to date this pavement on the basis of its form, since there are many similar pavements in Jerusalem, from the Herodian period and later, down to Byzantine times. Thus, our conclusion is drawn from two other details — the vaulted pool beneath it — the "Struthion Pool", and the triumphal arch above, the famous "Ecce Homo" arch. There is no doubt that the pavement is contemporaneous with the vaults beneath. The vaults themselves and the parallels given by Sister

Model of "Antonia Fortress" at Convent of Notre Dame de Sion

Marie-Aline de Sion would again point to the period of Hadrian.

According to Josephus (*War* V, 467), it appears that during the siege of 70 C.E. the Struthion Pool was still an open reservoir, for Titus built a ramp through it to gain access to the wall of Antonia for his battering-rams. It is thus clear that the Antonia fortress did not include this pool.

Another point of departure for the date of the pavement lies in the relationship between it and the Roman arch at its eastern side. The excavators ascribed this arch to the reign of Hadrian, who erected many such triumphal arches throughout the empire. If the pavement were Herodian, the piers of the arch — built some 160 years later — should rest upon the slabs of the pavement. Père Vincent and Sister Marie-Aline affirm that this was so, but in the 1966 excavations there it was revealed that the northern pier of the arch is built on bedrock. The rock itself was carefully hewn, so that the upper edge of the pavement slab adjacent to the pier touches the lower edge of the lowest course of the pier. Thus, it is quite clear that the architect who built the arch was also responsible for the laying of the pavement.

(B) **The gate and galleries.** Clarifying the relationship between the arch and the pavement is connected with the investigation of the form of the "western gate", which Père Vincent and Sister Marie-Aline regarded as the gate of the Antonia fortress. This is a monumental gate, 16 metres long and 16 metres wide, with two arched openings separated by a central pier; the eastern side of this pier comes to within 4 metres of the triumphal arch, which blocks the line of its central opening. It is untenable that both these gates were in contemporaneous use, and there is also no possibility of overcoming this difficulty by assuming that the gate of the fortress was built in Herodian times whereas the arch was built some 160 years later. It is unlikely that the Hadrianic architect would leave the ruins of a gate from the Herodian period blocking the opening of his arch. Thus, there is only one solution; the construction generally regarded as "Herodian" is actually much later — Byzantine, or possibly even Medieval.

Still easier to prove as baseless is the reconstruction of the "eastern gate" and "postern"; these gates are entirely hypothetical, based on the very unlikely assumption that there had been a way through the fortress to the Kidron valley beyond. Is it possible that Herod — followed by the Romans — would allow the people of Jerusalem to pass through the courtyard of the citadel on their way to the Kidron?

As for the galleries which supposedly adorned the courtyard called "Lithostrotos" — those on the south and west are pure reconstruction, with no archaeological foundation whatsoever. Proof of the existence of such a gallery on the east was sought in the remains of a stylobate discovered *in situ* in the Convent of the Flagellation, but P. Bagatti has proven that the stylobate was never part of a gallery. The northern gallery is represented by column bases, but these seem to be in secondary use there. In any event, the "gallery" around them was so poorly constructed that it is impossible to attribute them to a fortress of the Herodian period.

(C) The four "towers" so impressively reconstructed in the models are also entirely without foundation. The south-eastern "tower" alone was actually the entire Antonia fortress, as proposed below. Of the south-western "tower", nothing in fact is known, and thus it cannot properly be restored. The existence of a north-western "tower" had been inferred from a few scarps in the bedrock; these are probably connected with preparatory work for construction of the Hadrianic forum here. The meagre traces on which this "tower" is based,

thought to be Herodian, are in fact from an altogether different period, as proved by P. Bagatti.

Actually, in this writer's opinion, the fortress of Antonia stood on the mass of rock where the Omariyya school stands today; that is, south of the spot generally assigned to it in the reconstructions. This mass of rock, measuring 120 × 45 metres, is not too small for such a fortress as described by Josephus. Dalman and Bagatti may have been correct in assuming that in the period of Herod the bedrock spread farther south, and that this area was then larger. The reduction of this rock mass to its present dimensions occurred, according to their theory, under the Romans (Dalman) or the Arabs (Bagatti).

The pavement within the Convent of the Sisters of Sion, as noted, was of a small Roman forum. When Hadrian built Aelia Capitolina, he founded in the east and the west of the city monumental building-complexes — forum-squares, ornamented with triumphal arches, with cisterns beneath. In the west of the city we know of a forum adjacent to which the Holy Sepulchre was built; its cistern is found within the Convent of St. Abraham, and its triumphal arch is within the Alexandrovsky Hospice. On the east, a similar complex was built, as reviewed above.

This interpretation, in the author's opinion, indeed suits the archaeological facts.

The Gate of the Essenes and the Temple Scroll

Y. Yadin

Josephus, in his description of the course of the "First Wall" (*War* V, 144 ff.), states that the wall ran to the "Gate of the Essenes"; this is noteworthy not only because of the very name, but also because it has whetted the interest of the scholarly world concerning its exact location.

A particular passage in the Temple Scroll seems to throw light on both the existence and the location of this gate. In dealing with the various prohibitions concerning the "City of the Temple", the scroll decrees that the location of the public latrines was to be northwest of the city, and that they should be built in such a manner that the sewage would drain into pits. The place had to be roofed over so

Location of Gate of Essenes: (1) according to M. Avi-Yonah; (2) according to Y. Yadin; (3) assumed location of "Betso"

that the sewage should not be exposed within 3000 cubits of the city. The commandment in the Scroll: "And you shall make for them a place for the 'hand' outside the city to which they will go out," is based on Deuteronomy 23:12–14:

> You shall have a place outside the camp and you shall go out to it; and you shall have a stick with your weapons; and when you sit down outside, you shall dig a hole with it, and turn back and cover up your excrement. Because the Lord your God walks in the midst of your camp ..., therefore your camp must be holy, and that he may not see anything indecent among you.

A similar rule is found in the War Scroll, though there there it concerns latrines in an army camp during war: "And there shall be between all their camps and the place of the 'hand' about two thousand cubits, and no unseemly evil thing shall be seen in the vicinity of their encampments" (VII: 6–7). This is not the place to deal with the interesting problem of why the Sect fixed the distance in the camp as 2000 cubits, whereas in the "City of the Temple" the distance is 3000 cubits (treated partly in the author's commentary on the War Scroll, and to be dealt with in detail in his forthcoming edition of the Temple Scroll). For our present discussion, the important fact is that the Sect held that the "camp" of Deuteronomy is the "camp of Israel" in its entirety, identical according to their concept with "the entire City of the Temple". The "camp" mentioned in Deuteronomy has been interpreted by the Rabbinical Sages in a different manner, of course. In certain cases, the "camp" referred only to the encampment with the Tabernacle; in others, the Levite encampment, or in a very few cases, the entire Israelite encampment.

From the definition of the camp found in the Temple Scroll, it clearly emerges that the Sect conceived that not only were the latrines to be fixed outside the city, but that they were to be placed at some distance from it, to the northwest. Did the Sectarians indeed "practise" what they preached? The answer to this of course involves the identification of the Sect. Most scholars dealing with the Dead Sea Scrolls accept the view that the Sect is to be identified with the Essenes (as does the present author), known especially from Josephus and Philo of Alexandria. In describing the orthodoxy of the Essenes in keeping the Sabbath, Josephus writes:

> ... but [on the Sabbath] they will not remove any vessel out of its place, nor go to stool thereon. Nay, on other days they dig a small pit, a foot deep, with a paddle...and covering themselves round with their garment, that they may not affront the divine rays of light, they ease themselves into that pit, after which they put the earth that was dug out again into the pit; and even this they do only in the more lonely places, which they choose out for this purpose. (*War* II, 147-149 — Whiston translation).

This impartial description clearly indicates that the Essenes habitually "went out" to an open place, as specified in the Pentateuch, and for this purpose fixed a place outside the "camp" for their latrines.

In the light of this fact, we can assume that also the Essenes living in Jerusalem (Josephus often mentions them) upheld this practice. And now we see that the Temple Scroll fixed the location of the latrines of the "City of the Temple" to the northwest. Could this in some way be connected with the matter of the "Gate of the Essenes" in Jerusalem? Before answering this directly, we must review Josephus' description of the course of the "First Wall". According to him, the northern stretch of the wall ran from the north-western corner of the city eastward (from near today's "David's Tower") towards the Temple. He then describes the western stretch, from his previous starting point: "But if we go the other way westward, it began at the same place [near "David's Tower"], and extended through a place called 'Betso', to the gate of the Essenes." Finally, Josephus describes the southern and eastern stretches. We thus see that there are two specific loci in the western stretch, from north to south: "Betso", and the "Gate of the Essenes", according to the

description, both sites located quite close together.

The key to understanding this is the mysterious "Betso", with which scholars have often contended. The first to suggest that "Betso" should be interpreted as *beth-soa*, or "latrine", was the 19th century Jewish scholar J. Schwartz:[*] "The location of Bethsoa is unknown in all the studies of Palestine ... and in my opinion the location of the Bethsoa mentioned [by Josephus] is to be found there [i.e. in the area of the "Upper Pool"]. The American scholar E. Robinson also made this ascription, but held that it referred to the "Dung Gate". The German scholar G. Dalman followed Robinson, but regarded the name as connected indeed with latrines which had stood at an isolated place. Various other scholars located the "Gate of the Essenes" in the south-eastern corner of the city on this same basis.[**] In this spirit Avi-Yonah saw a possibility of explaining the existence of a gate with this name; "The Gate of the Essenes undoubtedly led to the principal settlement of this sect in the Judean Desert, that is, it is to be identified with the gate exiting upon the Kidron valley towards En-Rogel".[***] But such a location contradicts Josephus (who places both the gate and "Betso" along the western wall).

Returning to the Temple Scroll, the Beth-soa of the "City of the Temple" should be located northwest of the city. This direction would be quite suitable for the location of "Betso" (=*Beth-soa*), which should lie on the western side not far from the "Hippicus" tower at the northwest. If this suggested identification is correct, then the "Betso" mentioned by Josephus would be identical, in location and in function, with the "latrines" mentioned in the Temple Scroll.

This may also serve to explain the location of the "Gate of the Essenes" along the western stretch of the city-wall. The ancient inhabitants of Jerusalem would have seen Essenes leaving the walled city through a postern on this flank, in order to "ease" themselves. Thus (though the above must remain in the realm of the hypothetical) this gate, used by the Essenes daily, came to be named after them — an unofficial appellation not preserved in other sources.

[*] *Tevuot Haares*, ed. Lunz, Jerusalem, 1900, p. 335 (Hebrew).
[**] Cf,, e.g., M. Avi-Yonah: *Sefer Yerushalayim* I, map 10 following p. 312 (Hebrew).
[***] *Ibid.*, p. 307.

THE MEDIEVAL CITY

The Islamic Architecture of Jerusalem

M. Rosen-Ayalon

Jerusalem occupies the third position among the holy cities of Islam, only Mecca and Medina preceding it. This was clear already in the 7th century C.E.; there appears to have been a rather modest, plain building for the use of the faithful on the Temple Mount already in the days of Omar.* The French pilgrim Arculf, who visited Jerusalem around 670

* A survey of the monuments on the Temple Mount is currently being carried out under the direction of the author, on behalf of the Hebrew University in Jerusalem.

Air view of Temple Mount, looking southwest

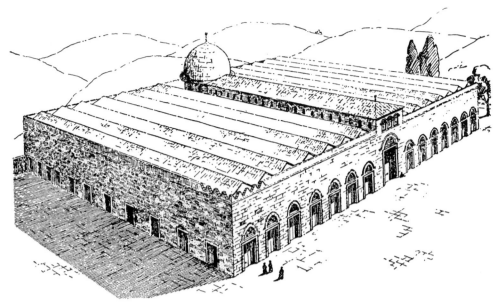

Reconstruction of original el-Aqsa mosque, 8th century C.E.

C.E., relates that this mosque could hold 3000 worshippers. It seems to have stood on the site of the present el-Aqsa mosque.

The Dome of the Rock (completed in 691/92 C.E.) was erected not as a mosque but as a shrine, to protect the holy rock located beneath its dome; this led to its name, *Qubbet es-Sahra* ("the Dome of the Rock"). The outer walls of this octagonal building enclose a double ambulatory, with a sort of inner octagon of arches between, rising above corner piers, and supporting a sloped roof; between each pair of piers are two columns. Above the central ring of arches, surrounding the rock, rises a large drum, pierced with windows and topped by the dome proper. Each of the eight external walls is pierced by windows. In the four walls of the cardinal directions, there are main doors. In spite of numerous repairs, modifications and renovations in the architectural ornamentation and in the dome, the plan is preserved in its initial state, with the original harmony and architectural conception intact. Various means of ornamentation, bright colours and rich patterns cover the interior; this is enhanced by an artistic-archaeological dimension, for most of the architectural ornamentation of the 7th century C.E. is still extant. Thus, we can see a blend of two imperial styles — Byzantine and Sassanid. The interior walls are faced with marble slabs, arranged to form patterns with the veins of the stone. Above the coloured marble columns are gilt Corinthian and Composite capitals; all the arches rising above the

middle octagon and the central circle are covered entirely with glass mosaics. The interior of the drum is also ornamented with mosaics. In these mosaics we find, alongside floral, naturalistic and abstract motifs, jewellery motifs such as gem-encrusted caskets, pendants, necklaces, pearl fringes and splendid crowns (see Pl. IV).

The situation is quite different with el-Aqsa mosque. It appears that the Caliph Walid I (705–715 C.E.), son of Abd el-Malik, erected this structure on the site of the first, crude building. Later in the 8th century C.E., after an earthquake, the mosque had to be rebuilt almost entirely. The historical sources indicate that the plan of the mosque included a nave and seven parallel aisles on either side. Slightly before the *mihrab* there was a dome, and it is most probable that it is this latter part only which has still preserved its original proportions today. From the 8th century C.E. we have a collection of carved wooden panels (some are on display at the Rockefeller Museum) which had been affixed to the joints of the tie beams between the arches. This large and rare group of richly ornamented objects is the best example of the woodwork of the first century of Islam.

In the Omayyad period, the walls of Jerusalem were strengthened, and a governor's palace (*Dar Imra*) was built (for the extensive Omayyad structures recently discovered near the Temple Mount, see below, pp. 97 ff.), Still, the prime importance of the city was religious. This is indicated by the very names of the city: *Beit el-Maqdas* ("the Temple", extended to the entire city), and *el-Quds* ("the Holy"), the name still employed today in Arabic. In that period, at the beginning of the 8th century C.E., Walid's brother, Suleiman, founded Ramla and fixed it as the administrative capital of the *Jund* of Falastin; thus, Jerusalem ceased to be the centre of authority in the country.

In the Abbasid period, el-Aqsa mosque was again rebuilt. In the 9th century C.E., the Caliph el-Ma'amun (the son of Harun er-Rashid) removed the name of Abd el-Malik from the dedicatory inscription in the mosaic of the Dome of the Rock, replacing it with his own. The contemporaneous Muslim historian el-Muqaddasi relates that at the start of the 10th century C.E. the mother of the Caliph el-Muqtader gave as a gift to the Dome of the Rock a set of carved wooden doors; in contrast, nothing is known of the construction of any significant new buildings in this period, and none such have survived.

The Fatimid Caliph ez-Zaher (1022–1023 C.E.) is to be credited with the reconstruction of the dome of the Dome of the Rock, as well as large parts of el-Aqsa mosque, as the building stands today, with its mosaics around the interior of the dome. The Fatimids also rebuilt the fortifications of the city, in 1033 and later, in 1063, but their internal conflicts led to the city's fall into the hands of the Seljuqs in 1071. Shortly after, on the eve of the arrival of the Crusaders, the Fatimids again reconquered the city.

Such literary sources as Muqaddasi, Nasir i Khosrau and others mention, in this period, monastery-like collective dwellings for Moslem clergy, hospitals, baths, public lavatories, a water-supply system and, of course, mosques. Even so, it appears that Jerusalem had not yet returned to its former splendour and was not the most important of the cities in this country.

After the Crusader conquest of Jerusalem, the Dome of the Rock became a Christian prayer-hall; the structure itself, however, was not particularly modified. The Templars erected an altar on the rock, and placed a cross at the top of the dome. In contrast, the Crusaders added considerable sections to the structure of el-Aqsa, mainly in the forepart of the building, and refurbished its façade.

Saladin, the Ayyubid who retook Jerusalem from the Crusaders in 1187, gave el-Aqsa mosque its splendid *minbar* ("pulpit"); this rare example of the skill of the Syrian woodworkers, great experts in their field, was unfortunately destroyed in the fire in the mosque in 1968.

The Moslem character of Jerusalem as we know it today appears largely to be the product of the Mamluk period, between the 13th and 16th centuries C. E. The Mamluks initiated and sponsored the erection of many buildings in the city, just as they did in many other cities within their realm. They built public, secular buildings of Moslem style (markets, *madrasas*, hospitals, etc.), and were active in the Haram esh-Sharif (Temple Mount) as well. It was in this period that a literature in praise of Jerusalem — *Fadail el-Quds* — was largely diffused by the Sufis of that age. Already at the end of the 13th century C.E. we find a sultan proud of his rule in Jerusalem. In the inscriptions of Baybars there appears the title *Sahb el-Qibletein*, "Lord of the Two *Qibles*", referring to Jerusalem and Mecca, the former being the first towards which the Prophet had prayed.

In the days of the Mamluk Sultan en-Nasr Muhammad bin Qala'un (1318–1319 C.E.), restoration work was carried out in the Dome of the Rock. It seems that at this time the series of central piers was covered with marble panelling, during which the mosaics along the edges of the arches were damaged. The marble is alternating black and white. Further, the ceiling of the outer ambulatory seems also to have been redone then, as was the inner lining of the dome. The corpus of ornamental, floral and calligraphic motifs from the Mamluk period was modelled in stucco and then painted, with highlights in gold, red and green on a white background. Part of the high windows remaining still today may have been made at this same time.

The topography of the Haram areas does not seem, generally, to have changed since the 15th century C.E. The matter of the gates of the Haram is a complicated one, and we have no detailed description of them prior to the 14th century C.E. Several of them were probably in existence already in the Fatimid period, and even these may well have stood on the sites of older gates, from the Omayyad period; a few could even stem from the Herodian Temple Mount. Several historians, such as Nasir i Khosrau and Mujir ed-Din, often mention

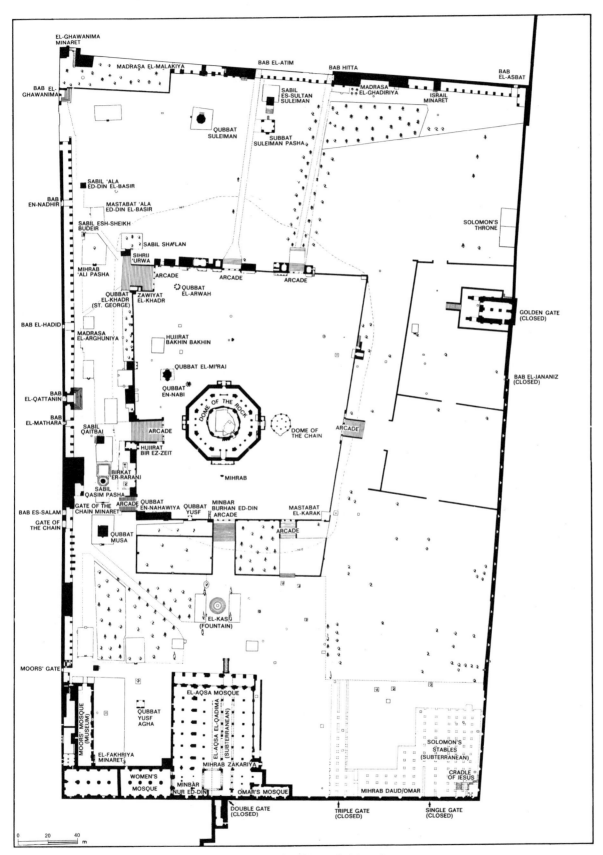

EL-GHAWANIMA
MINARET

MADRASA EL-MALAKIYA

BAB EL-ATIM

BAB HITTA

BAB
EL-ASBAT

BAB EL-
GHAWANIMA

SABIL
ES-SULTAN
SULEIMAN

MADRASA
EL-GHADIRIYA

ISRAIL
MINARET

QUBBAT
SULEIMAN

SUBBAT
SULEIMAN PASHA

BAB
EN-NADHIR

SABIL 'ALA
ED-DIN EL-BASIR

SOLOMON'S
THRONE

MASTABAT 'ALA
ED-DIN EL-BASIR

SABIL ESH-SHEIKH
BUDEIR

SABIL SHA'LAN

SIHRIJ
'URWA

MIHRAB
'ALI PASHA

ARCADE

ARCADE

ARCADE

QUBBAT
EL-KHADR
(ST. GEORGE)

ZAWIYAT
EL-KHADR

QUBBAT
EL-ARWAH

BAB EL-HADID

MADRASA
EL-ARGHUNIYA

HUJIRAT
BAKHIN BAKHIN

GOLDEN GATE
(CLOSED)

QUBBAT EL-MI'RAJ

BAB
EL-QATTANIN

QUBBAT
EN-NABI

BAB EL-JANANIZ
(CLOSED)

BAB
EL-MATHARA

DOME OF THE ROCK

SABIL
QAITBAI

ARCADE

ARCADE

DOME OF
THE CHAIN

HUJIRAT
BIR EZ-ZEIT

BIRKAT
'ER-RARANJ

MIHRAB

SABIL
QASIM PASHA

BAB ES-SALAM

GATE OF THE
CHAIN MINARET

ARCADE

QUBBAT
EN-NAHAWIYA

QUBBAT
YUSF

MINBAR
BURHAN ED-DIN
ARCADE

MASTABAT
EL-KARAK

GATE OF
THE CHAIN

QUBBAT
MUSA

ARCADE

MOORS' GATE

EL-KAS
(FOUNTAIN)

EL-AQSA MOSQUE

MOORS' MOSQUE (MUSEUM)

QUBBAT
YUSF
AGHA

EL-AQSA EL-QADIMA
(SUBTERRANEAN)

SOLOMON'S
STABLES
(SUBTERRANEAN)

EL-FAKHRIYA
MINARET

CRADLE
OF JESUS

MIHRAB ZAKARIYA

WOMEN'S
MOSQUE

MINBAR
NUR ED-DIN

OMAR'S MOSQUE

MIHRAB DAUD/OMAR

0   20   40
m

DOUBLE GATE
(CLOSED)

TRIPLE GATE
(CLOSED)

SINGLE GATE
(CLOSED)

Haram esh-Sharif (Temple Mount)

gates along the various walls of the Haram (for instance, the Western Wall), but not always are the names the same.

The Sultan Tunkiz (A.H. 712–740) renovated el-Aqsa mosque and added other structures such as the water installations near Jerusalem, the minaret near Bab es-Silsile ("Gate of the Chain"), a *madrasa* and dwellings, and a bazaar, hospice and baths. In the mid-15th century C.E. a sort of open "summer mosque" was built on the upper area above the stairs leading to el-Aqsa mosque, named after the Qadi Burhan ed-Din. This Mamluk monument, entirely of marble, contains all the basic elements of a mosque: the *mihrab* (prayer niche) on the southern wall, with a *minbar* constructed of marble, its stairs with ornamented marble balustres and its platform, where the preacher stood, crowned by a small cupola.

In the second half of the 15th century the Mamluk Sultan Qaitbai erected a fountain (*sabil*) near the Dome of the Rock. This is a small structure, square in plan with engaged columns at the corners, supporting a slightly pointed dome, the surface of the latter entirely carved with delicate tendrils and arabesques.

Already in the 15th century C.E. there seem to have been eight stairways leading from the lower Haram, on which el-Aqsa stands, up to the level of the platform bearing the Dome of the Rock. At the top of each of these stairways is an arcade (of varying numbers of arches); these form "gates" known in Arabic as *mawazin*, "scales". The arches and their carved ornamentation are not all contemporaneous, nor are the capitals. Most are from the Mamluk period, but parts are earlier (Ayyubid) or later (Ottoman).

The Ottoman period contributed the mighty fortification system, much of which still stands in its original state, built by the 16th century C.E. Otto-man Sultan Suleiman the Magnificent. The lines of this city-wall appear to follow those of the Fatimid period. Suleiman also showed concern for the Dome of the Rock; in his day the eight external walls, from beneath the windows to the roof, were faced with colourful glazed tiles (from the base of the structure up to the beginning of these tiles the walls are faced with marble panelling). These tiles replaced the original mosaic, the glass tesserae of which, exposed to the elements, had become damaged over the years. This led to a basic change in the character of the windows in these walls; on the basis of archaeological investigations, they originally had been similar to the known examples of Omayyad windows, outstandingly carved out from large marble plaques and holding panes of coloured glass (as found in the Great Mosque at Damascus, and very similar to the stucco examples from Khirbet Mefjer). Suleiman's artisans built double-walled windows: The outer wall was flush with the outer, tiled surface of the building's walls, the tiles covering the solid parts of the pierced window; the inner wall of the windows was built parallel, made of stucco inset with panes of coloured glass, as found in Ottoman mosques at other cities, such as at Istanbul.

In the 18th century C.E. the ceiling of the middle ambulatory of the Dome of the Rock was repaired. There are clear differences in style between the ornamentation of the dome and the outer ambulatory (painted stucco in Mamluk style), and that of the 18th century ceiling in the middle ambulatory.

The latest renovations in the Dome of the Rock were carried out in recent years by the Jordanian Government. The outer dome was rebuilt in anodized aluminium, and the glazed tiles of the exterior were replaced entirely, the previous ones from Suleiman's day having been in rather poor condition. The renovation of el-Aqsa mosque was also begun under Jordanian rule and is continuing.

The Area South of the Temple Mount in the Early Islamic Period

M. Ben-Dov

Already at the start of excavations south of the Southern Wall of the Temple Mount, it became evident that the area between the Turkish city-wall and the Southern Wall contained a very large building of some 7.5 dunams in area (84×96 m). The continuation of work to the west and north, west of the Western Wall, showed that this structure was not isolated, but was actually part of an extensive building-complex. Outside the present-day walls, structures of a similar character were also revealed. So far, six enormous buildings have been found, comprising a single complex. The plan of the largest of them, building II, closely resembles those of the palaces of the Omayyad period in this country, in Transjordan and in Syria. There are differences, however: In the palaces, there are towers at the corners and middle of the exterior walls, whereas here there are no exterior towers whatsoever (see below). The stratigraphic picture and the finds confirm this dating. Beneath the floors of the building and beneath the associated streets — houses, installations and channels came to light together with an abundance of finds including much pottery and thousands of coins, and stamped roof-tiles of the Byzantine period — all from late in that period. In the stratum above the building-complex, which was destroyed in a natural catastrophe and not rebuilt (see below), remains of a very meagre settlement of the 9th century C.E. were found amongst the ruins. The complex had been equipped with a broad, well-planned sewer network, which remained unknown to the people of the meagre settlement. Various finds came to light in this sewer network, which relate to the latest phase of its use, including complete pottery vessels of "Khirbet Mefjer ware", and coins of the 8th century C.E. This was a most important archaeological discovery, for it is the first time large structures of the Omayyad period (660–750 C.E.) were found outside the Haram esh-Sherif.

Our knowledge of the history of the country and its settlement in the Omayyad period is quite sporadic, especially concerning Jerusalem, and, in the light of our discoveries, it was decided to re-examine the walls and gates of the Temple Mount, especially the Southern Wall and the "Double Gate". This has revealed an entirely new picture of the area.

At the end of the Byzantine period, a residential quarter lay adjacent to the walls of the Temple Mount, which appear to have towered to their full height at that time. This quarter included public buildings, and private houses of one and two storeys, with open areas between utilized for gardening. The Parthian conquest of Jerusalem in 614 C.E. also left its imprint here. The Southern Wall was especially damaged, a large breach having been forced. During the Byzantine reconquest, and early in the period of the Arab conquest, no significant changes seem to have taken place in this area,

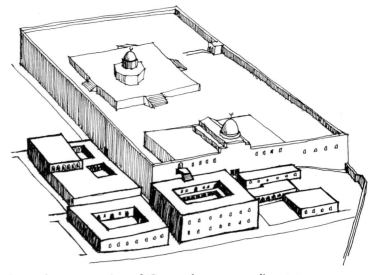

Isometric reconstruction of Omayyad structures adjacent to Temple Mount

Air view of Omayyad structures adjacent to Temple Mount, during excavations

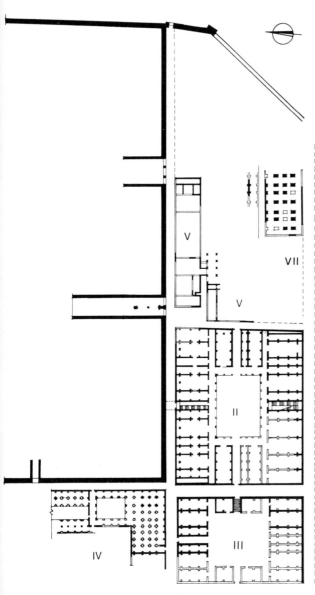

Plan of Omayyad structures adjacent to Temple Mount

is based largely on the evidence of a bridge which had connected the roof of building II with el-Aqsa mosque, spanning the street running along the Southern Wall and enabling direct access from the roof of the building into the mosque. It is assumed that the place was erected by the Caliph el-Walid I (705–715 C.E.). In the centre of the structure is an enclosed courtyard, surrounded by porticoes. The foundations of the exterior and interior walls are deeply set and very massive, often reaching 9 m below the floor-level. The roof had rested upon stone arches or on thick wooden beams supported by pillars. The existence of a second storey in building II is indicated by the level of the abovementioned bridge, as well as by a system of drain-pipes lying within the walls, leading to the central sewers beneath the groundfloor-level. There seem to have been various installations in this upper storey, such as kitchens and toilets.

Besides the sewer network, building II had an intricate system, drawing rainwater from the roofs and from the courtyard to large cisterns. These cisterns also received water from the main Jerusalem aqueduct.

The floors of building II are paved with square flagstones laid over a thick layer of fill — sometimes reaching 4.5 m in thickness. This fill includes mainly debris from the immediate area and from the construction of the building itself; within it have been found installations for mixing plaster and the like. It should be remembered that the builders first erected the skeleton of the entire building, and then plastered the walls; only in the final stages of work was the floor laid. During construction, the skeleton was used as dwelling quarters for the workers; this can serve to explain many of the remains within the fill. The flagstones were laid directly on a thin layer of *terra rosa* (15–20 cm thick), overlying the fill.

We have already noted the lack of towers in the structures before us — in contrast to other Omayyad palaces. This would seem to be of aid in determining the purpose of such towers in general. It is usually considered that the Omayyad builders derived their basic palace plan from the Byzantine fortress plan, giving the towers no specific function. That they were indeed intended for defence, however, in the isolated palaces, is indicated by their very absence in the Jerusalem structures, which were within the

occurring only under the Omayyad caliphs, who established an extensive religious centre in Jerusalem. Of this project we had known only of the structures within the Haram: the Dome of the Rock, el-Aqsa mosque and other smaller monuments. We now know that the large breach in the Southern Wall was repaired by the planners of the entire Omayyad complex, and that the "Double Gate" in its present form was also built by them.

The six structures uncovered were planned as a complex in conjunction with the Temple Mount. As noted, the outstanding structure is building II, which we have defined as a palace. This definition

Eastern gate of Omayyad building II, blocked by foundations of Turkish city-wall above

function of each of the several structures, but it can be assumed that the palace and the surrounding complex included a bathing establishment (apparently now being uncovered) and dwelling quarters for distinguished visitors.

From among the plethora of finds from these buildings, we may note the large number of architectural fragments — capitals, friezes, architraves and balustres, as well as fresco fragments and some stucco-work. Among the many pottery types of this period, most notable are the zoomorphic and glazed vessels, which already began making their appearance in this country at this time. Many

Omayyad orthostat (above) and capital (below) from building II

city's walled perimeter and thus required no defences of their own.

The simplicity of the gates of our buildings is in decided contrast to the architectural splendour of the palace gates at other Omayyad sites. Further, the architectural elements and painted plaster fragments found in our structures contain only geometric and floral designs, again in contrast to the palaces outside Jerusalem, where faunal and human motifs abound — often in quite bold scenes. The "Double Gate" in its Omayyad form is also outstanding in its simplicity, artistically and architecturally. This austerity was most probably motivated by the sanctity of Jerusalem, though our structures may represent an architectural phase preceding that of the ornamented palaces.

The five other buildings around building II have only incompletely been excavated, and thus their full study remains for the future. For the time, we may note that several of them are similar in plan (but not identical) to the palace, whereas several others are of an entirely different plan. A few are pillared buildings, with large, roofed-over areas; others are reminiscent of khans with broad enclosed courtyards surrounded by chambers. All these structures have complex water, drainage and sewage systems. It is still impossible to determine the

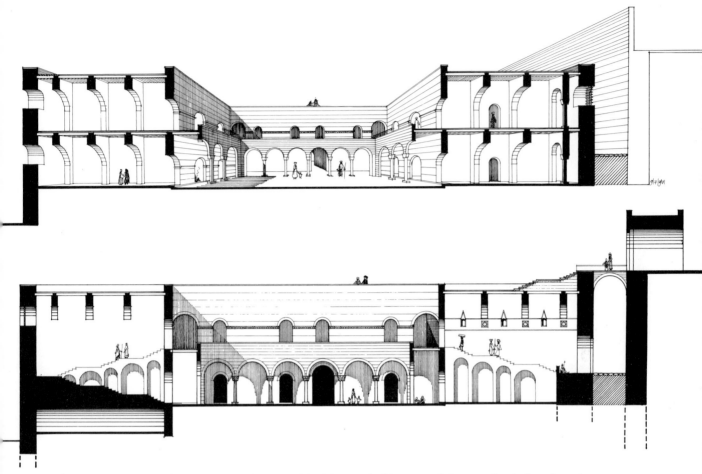

Above: sectional view through centre of Omayyad building II, looking west; below: sectional view through western part of building II, looking west

gold, silver and bronze coins have come to light, mostly struck at Ramla and Jerusalem ("Aelia", on the coins), and some from Damascus. Glassware, metal objects and bone implements also were found.

The building-complex was destroyed by a heavy earthquake, traces of which can still be observed. This was the disastrous quake of 747/48 C.E., which hit Jerusalem especially hard; Talmudic literature denotes this catastrophe as the "quake in the sabbatical year".

The area was not renewed in its former plan after the disaster, and the rise of the Abbasids put an end to Omayyad aspirations for Jerusalem. Not only were no renovations or construction carried out here, but the ruins became a huge quarry, a source for building stone for anyone needing such material. In the 11th century it served as a cemetery, indicating that the immense complex which had stood here was entirely forgotten. The history of the site in Abbasid through Ottoman times reflects its wretched state. From time to time, ripples of activity were felt here, but the few structures which rose over the ruins were of a private nature, and the area never recovered its former splendour.

Jerusalem in Crusader Days

J. Prawer

When the Crusaders placed Jerusalem under siege on July 15, 1099, they found before them a fortified city with an Egyptian occupation force stationed in the Citadel, the Muslim and Jewish inhabitants planted on the walls in their respective quarters, and the Eastern Christian population — the "Assyrians", suspected of sympathy with the Crusader attackers — expelled. In general terms, the walls enclosing the city were built upon the line usually ascribed to Aelia Capitolina, the Roman colony. Basically, this line remained unchanged throughout the period of Crusader rule. In the time of Saladin (1187–1192) and a generation later, in the days of Frederick II (after 1229), an attempt was made to expand the walls by including the plateau of Mount Zion.

The internal street network also survived from Roman times. The main street from north to south (from Damascus Gate to Zion Gate) and the intersecting street running from east to west (St. Stephan's Gate to Jaffa Gate), divided the city into four quarters: Already at the end of the Arab period each of these quarters had taken on a religious-ethnic character of its own. The north-western quarter, around the Church of the Holy Sepulchre, was settled by the various Eastern Christian sects; the north-eastern quarter was settled by the Jews; two southern quarters, adjacent to the Citadel and the Temple Mount respectively, were Muslim neighbourhoods.

Upon the Crusader conquest, the population of the city changed drastically. The Muslim and Jewish inhabitants were slaughtered (in July 1099) and it was with great difficulty that the new Crusader population was able to fill even a single quarter; naturally, the new inhabitants concentrated around the Church of the Holy Sepulchre and the Citadel. The Crusaders resorted to special inducements, such as customs exemptions and cancellation of property ownership in cases of absentee owners, to attract settlers to the city. This filled the former Jewish Quarter with a Christian Assyrian populace, though the quarter still preserved its former name — "Juiverie". By law, Jews and Muslims were forbidden to settle there, for their presence was thought to defile the city's sanctity. The inhabitants of Jerusalem in the 12th century were mostly Europeans. During the entire existence of the Crusader state, France was the prime source for Crusader manpower, though other nationalities also settled in the city. The fact that French was the official language brought about the concentration of linguistic "minorities" in certain streets, where the newly arrived settler could keep his customary way of life. Thus, the German speakers established their own branch of the Hospitallers in the area between the Temple Mount and Zion Gate; the Hungarians concentrated around their own hospice not far from the present-day New Gate; the Spaniards had a street near the Damascus Gate; and the Provençals concentrated west of Zion Gate.

If this was the situation amongst the Europeans, it was even more so among the Eastern Christians. The "Assyrians" settled in the then Jewish Quarter, but the other Eastern Christians concentrated around the sites of their various churches which they had built long before the Crusader conquest. Thus, the Copts were to be found near the Church of St. Mary Magdalena (near Herod's Gate); and the Greek Orthodox, who had been stripped of most of their churches by the Latin Crusaders, but retained rights in the Holy Sepulchre and several other churches, concentrated around the monastery and hospice of Mar Saba, opposite the Citadel. The important Armenian community, which in the 7th century began building monasteries and hospices with the support of their kings in far-off Armenia, gave its name to an entire neighbourhood around the Church of St. James, near Zion Gate. The

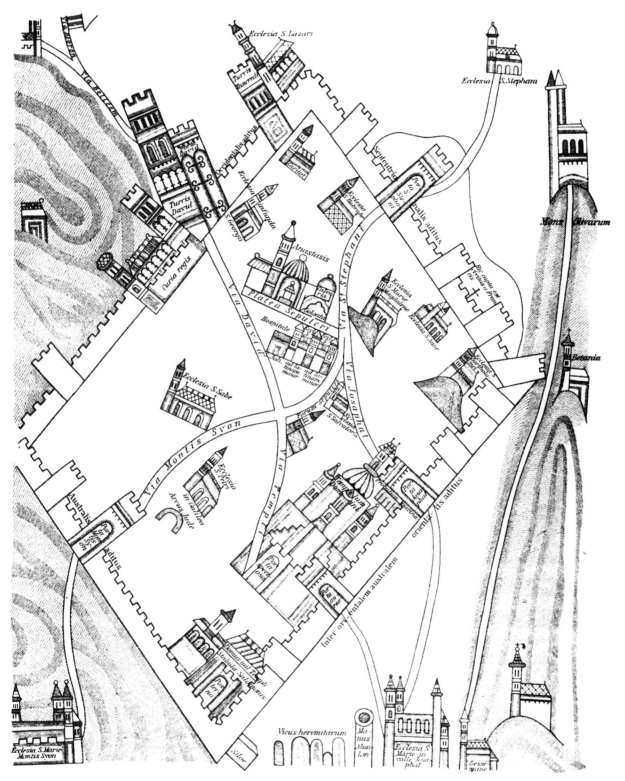

Twelfth century map of Jerusalem (Cambrai MS)

Church of St. Abraham, near Damascus Gate, may also have belonged to the Copts; and the Church of the Cross, far outside the walls to the west was in the hands of the Georgians.

Defence of the city was based on three factors: on the city fortifications; the official occupation troops; the forces of the various military orders and general conscription of the inhabitants in time of emergency. The city fortifications comprised the line of the walls, more than four kilometres long. The especially weak points along this line were the stretch crossing the upper part of Mount Zion; the north-western part of the city; and the stretch between Damascus Gate and the north-eastern corner of the city. The Crusaders sought to strengthen these points by bringing Mount Zion within the walls, by providing deeper fosses before the walls, and by building outworks. The main fortification of the city was the Citadel, which over the years came to bear the name "David's Tower". The Crusaders here utilized the foundations of Herod's towers, previously incorporated within the defences of Aelia Capitolina and its Byzantine successor. The Crusaders, however, expanded the Citadel to the south. A fortress in itself, and surrounded by its own fosse, it joined the city fosse, but jutted into the city proper, with only a bridge connecting it with the city. On the south the Citadel adjoined the royal Crusader palace, apparently built on the podium of Herod's palace, up to a now-blocked gate in the modern wall, opposite the end of Armenian Patriarchate Street, facing Mount Zion.

Besides Jaffa Gate, the principal entrance to the city was through the then "St. Stephan's Gate" (Damascus Gate), named after the church opposite this gate, outside the walls. It was from this direction that most of the pilgrims arrived from the coastal plain, by way of Ramla, Latrun, Qubeibe and Nebi Samwil. The third most important gate was "Zion Gate", slightly east of its modern successor. In the eastern wall of the city there was "Jehosaphat's Gate" (today's St. Stephan's Gate), leading out to the Kidron ("Jehosaphat") valley. The "Golden Gate", in the Eastern Wall of the Temple Mount, was opened only once annually, in honour of the religious procession coming from the Mount of Olives; the "Tanner's Gate" (modern Dung Gate) was on the south; the "Beaucaire Gate", at the end of Armenian Patriarchate Street, was named

after the Provençal Crusaders who camped there with their commander, Raymond of St. Gilles. In the northern wall there were also two posterns, "St. Lazar" (near the modern New Gate; named after the Order of Lepers on the site), and "Magdalena" (in the inner cross-wall at the north-eastern corner of the city, which ran between the northern and eastern walls near Burj el-Laqlaq; see map, p. 115).

Three military orders concentrated their forces here in Jerusalem. The Templars converted el-Aqsa mosque and the southern part of the Temple Mount into their abode, and turned the subterranean areas below into stables — the splendid "Solomon's Stables" still visible today. The Hospitallers had their centre near the Holy Sepulchre; there also were the dwelling-quarters and hospitals of the Order. The name "Muristan", today applied to the relatively recent market (built at the start of the present century) adjacent to the Holy Sepulchre, is actually a corruption of the Persian word *bimeristan* "hospital". Another order, that of the Lepers of St. Lazar, was located near the modern New Gate. The Teutonic Knights, who in the 12th century were merely a branch of the Hospitallers, were centred in the area of the modern Jewish Quarter.

Churches

As the capital of the Crusader kingdom, Jerusalem contained the main administative institutions of the state. Moreover, its religious character made it a city not merely with many churches, but rather a city of religious institutions and, above all, a city of pilgrims from all Christendom.

Most of the important churches were located along the axis descending from the summit of the Mount of Olives, crossing the Kidron valley and rising through "Jehosaphat's Gate", along the street known in Crusader times as "Jehosaphat Street", running west till it reached the Holy Sepulchre. Churches were also concentrated on Mount Zion and the Temple Mount, though these were of lesser importance.

Most of the Crusader churches are built over Byzantine structures, or nearby Byzantine sites; e.g. the Church of the Ascension on the Mount of Olives; and the Church of Gethsemane, where Jesus was arrested. In contrast, in the Kidron valley there is a well-preserved church, the Church of the Tomb of the Blessed Virgin (or St. Mary of the

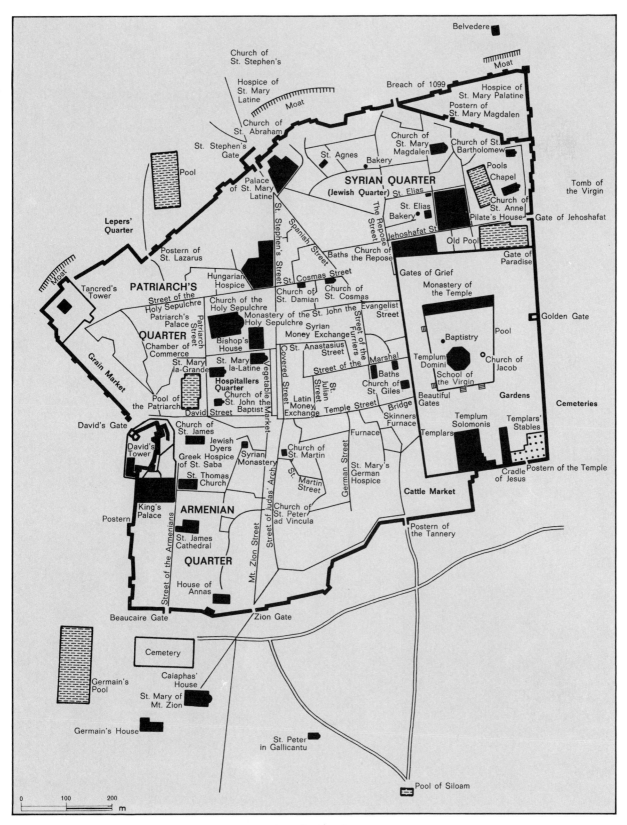

Belvedere

Church of
St. Stephen's

Moat

Hospice of
St. Mary
Latine

Breach of 1099

Hospice of
St. Mary Palatine

Moat

Postern of
St. Mary Magdalen

Church of
St. Abraham

St. Stephen's
Gate

Church of
St. Mary
Magdalen

Church of St.
Bartholomew

St. Agnes

Bakery

Pool

Palace
of St. Mary
Latine

SYRIAN QUARTER

(Jewish Quarter) St. Elias

Pools

Chapel

Church of
St. Anne

Tomb of
the Virgin

Lepers'
Quarter

St. Elias
Bakery

Pilate's House

Gate of Jehoshafat

Jehoshafat St.

Postern of
St. Lazarus

The Repose Street

Old Pool

Gate of
Paradise

Moat

Tancred's
Tower

PATRIARCH'S

Street of the
Holy Sepulchre

Patriarch's
Palace

QUARTER

Chamber of
Commerce

Hungarian
Hospice

Church of the
Holy Sepulchre

Spanish Street

St. Stephen's Street

Baths

St. Cosmas Street

Church of
St. Damian

Church of
St. Cosmas

Church of the
Repose

Gates of Grief

Monastery of
the Temple

Gate of
Paradise

Monastery of the
Holy Sepulchre

St. John the Evangelist
Street

Bishop's
House

Syrian
Money Exchange

St. Anastasius
Street

Baptistry

Pool

St. Mary
la-Grande

St. Mary
la-Latine

Street of the Furriers

Street of the

Marshal

Templum
Domini

Church of
Jacob

Golden Gate

Patriarch Street

Covered Street

Hospitallers
Quarter

Church of
St. John the
Baptist

Vegetable Market

Latin
Money
Exchange

Baths

St. Julian Street

Church of
St. Giles

School of
the Virgin

Grain Market

Pool of
the Patriarch

David Street

Temple Street

Beautiful
Gates

Gardens

Cemeteries

David's Gate

Church of
St. James

Jewish
Dyers

Syrian
Monastery

Church of
St. Martin

Bridge

Skinners
Furnace

Templum
Solomonis

Templars'
Stables

David's
Tower

Greek Hospice
of St. Saba

St. Thomas
Church

St. Martin
Street

Furnace

German Street

St. Mary's
German
Hospice

Templars

Cradle
of Jesus

Postern of the Temple

King's
Palace

ARMENIAN

Street of Judas' Arch

St.

Cattle Market

Postern

St. James
Cathedral

QUARTER

Mt. Zion Street

Church of
St. Peter
ad Vincula

Postern of
the Tannery

Street of the Armenians

House of
Annas

Beaucaire Gate

Zion Gate

Cemetery

Germain's
Pool

Caiaphas'
House

St. Mary of
Mt. Zion

Germain's House

St. Peter
in Gallicantu

Pool of Siloam

0   100   200
                m

Crusader Jerusalem

105

Façade of St. Anne's Church

Valley of Jehosaphat), containing the tombs of the Crusader kings of Jerusalem, including Queen Millicent (1101–1161), the wife of Fulk of Anjou. The entrance to this church is Romanesque in style (ca. 1130).

The most beautiful of all the Crusader churches in Jerusalem, however, is that of St. Anne (the house of Anne and Joachim, the Virgin Mary's parents). This church belonged to the Benedictine Sisters and received royal support. The building is an admirable product of the Romanesque art of the mid-12th century. It is basilical (34 × 19.5 metres), the nave being slightly wider than the two side aisles. A clerestory lights the nave; the aisles receive light from a row of pointed windows in the outer walls of the building. The main splendour of the church is in the portal and the upper window on the façade. The entire Church of St. Anne is built in a delicate style, ornamented within and without to the point of being a Romanesque showpiece; indeed, it is one of the highlights of Crusader architecture.

Whereas the Crusader architects could build the Church of St. Anne almost without regard for earlier structures on the site, they met with extreme difficulties in restoring the Church of the Holy Sepulchre. The Crusader architects were faced with two major problems; restoring the several elements and building an overall structure which could contain them — all shrines connected with the final hours in the life of Jesus. Most of these elements dated to the 4th century C.E., built under the patronage of the Empress Helena and repaired 200 years later, under Justinian. The Persian invasion and the Arab conquest (7th century) had wrought havoc on them and they had been restored since only in part; in the 7th century (by the Patriarch Modestus); in the mid-11th century (under the patronage of the Byzantine Emperor Constantine Monomachus); and after 1010 C.E. The Crusaders solved the problem of an overall structure, in part by exploiting the existing structures and in part by adding construction where it was lacking. Besides this, however, they were faced with integrating the existing with the new within a single, unified structure.

The earlier structures incorporated within the building were at the western and eastern extremities. At the western end was the splendid Byzantine structure known as the "Anastasis", that is, the

Portal of Church of Holy Sepulchre

"Church of the Resurrection" (also called the "Rotunda", built over the "Tomb of Jesus"). The Crusaders added to it on the east, erecting a basilical structure with four aisles, which continued beyond the church and took in the Chapel of Queen Helena and the Chapel of the Holy Cross. The raised chapel of Golgotha (Calvary), adjacent to the main portals, was also included. Though functionally successful, this integration certainly does not contribute to the beauty of the building, to its harmony or to its clarity of line. In compensation, the façade of the church befits the artistic abilities of those who undertook its erection. We do not know precisely how long the work continued, but it was completed in 1149, that is, fifty years after the Crusader Conquest of the city. The principal building operations probably began sometime in the 1130's.

Markets and Streets

The economic life of Crusader Jerusalem was entirely a consumer economy, centred around a series of markets near the Holy Sepulchre. From the viewpoint of the pilgrim, most important were the two centres of the money-changers—north of the city's markets, in a narrow street, were the Assyrian money-changers, while on the south, in a parallel street, were the Franks. The markets of Jerusalem are of quite early origin and in part stem from the Forum of Aelia Capitolina. The central market was Malcuisinat street, built around the middle of the 12th century by Queen Millicent. Many of the shops of this market belonged to the Church of St. Anne; indeed, the monogram of this church — "SA" — is still to be seen on many of of the shops. Here, amongst the stalls, stores and counters, the pilgrim could satisfy his culinary needs.

West of Malcuisinat street was the Spice-market or Vegetable-market, and to the east, the "Vaulted Street", containing, apparently, stalls with dry goods and textiles. To the north, in a narrow street separating the Holy Sepulchre from three churches opposite (the Hospitallers; "Maria latinam maior"; and "Maria latinam minor"), was Rue des Paumiers, where the pilgrim could purchase a palm-frond, the traditional symbol of the pilgrim to Jerusalem, as well as religious keepsakes, such as *ampulae* with holy water and, of course, numerous forms of crosses. There were also numerous "relics" for sale: stones which had touched Jesus' body, or from the Temple; bones or hair of Saints; and other items which could be taken back to Europe.

Adjacent to the Citadel was the wholesale market, extending from the region of Jaffa Gate to the large pool known then as the "Pool of the Patriarch" (Hezekiah's Pool). This was mainly a grain market; farther north was the pig market. A second commercial centre was southwest of the Temple Mount, in the area of the present Jewish Quarter. Here was the cattle-market, and nearby, naturally, were the workshops of the tanners and the butchers' stalls.

In the 12th century, though Jewish settlement was not renewed in Jerusalem, a few Jews did practice dyeing; they lived in the region of "David's Tower". Jewish settlement was revived early in the 13th century, especially after the coming of Nahmanides in 1267. A later tradition places the site of his academy in a synagogue near the ruined "Hurva" synagogue; but we cannot be sure just where the Jewish Quarter was prior to the 15th century.

Royal Crusader seal, inscribed: "City of the king, the king of kings"; in centre, from left to right, depictions of Holy Sepulchre, David's Tower and Dome of the Rock

Excavations at Tancred's Tower

D. Bahat and M. Ben-Ari

At the north-western corner of the Old City of Jerusalem there are the remains of a tower, built of very large stones. This often studied tower is generally called *Qasr Jalud* ("Goliath's Castle") by the Arabs or "Tancred's Tower" in most European sources.

The Russian pilgrim Father Daniel, who visited the Holy Land in 1106/1107, relates that a bow's shot away from David's Tower lies the spot where David killed Goliath. Several years later (in *ca.* 1130 C.E.) the site was visited by another pilgrim, Fetellus, who relates that between St. Stephan's Gate (today's Damascus Gate) and Tancred's Tower there stood a lepers' colony. The latter name also appears in the Cambrai map of the mid-12th century C.E., as the traditional site of David's slaying Goliath. It was here that Tancred breached the walls in 1099.

Even though many scholars were of the opinion that large parts of the tower were medieval, some persisted in ascribing them — or at least the foundations — to the period of the Second Temple. Some even attempted to identify them with the Psephinus Tower, described by Josephus as standing at the north-western corner of the Third Wall.*

Recently we had the opportunity to study the history of this structure more thoroughly.** Alongside work on the National Park adjacent to the Old City walls here, the Department of Antiquities and Museums conducted archaeological excavations immediately outside the city-wall. Work continued from November 1971 till April 1972, and revealed that the Turkish city-wall, running here from east to west, has left some 3 metres of the tower outside its line; it was principally these remains which were investigated.

Excavations in and under the foundations of the tower revealed that it was indeed built in the Middle Ages, for beneath the foundations was found pottery of that period. Thus, we have before us a large tower of about 35 × 35 metres, built throughout of huge ashlars from the Herodian period, here in secondary use, founded directly upon or slightly above bedrock.

North and west of the tower, a street ran between it and the then city-wall. This street was some 3 metres wide. Though parts of this city-wall were known previously, this is the first time that it was possible to determine, by means of sections, that this wall, which is some 3 metres thick, was built at the same time as the tower. It was protected on the outside by a quarried fosse, 19 metres wide in the part uncovered. We have not yet been able to determine its depth, though we have reached some 7 metres down.

* For a recent review of this subject, see M. Avi-Yonah: *IEJ* 18 (1968), pp. 103–105.

** A visit to the basement of the Christian Brothers College revealed that the tower set off at an angle near the south-western corner of Tancred's Tower, appearing in all the published plans of the tower, is most likely of later construction.

Plan of excavations at Tancred's Tower. Legend: A — aqueduct; CW — Crusader city-wall; TW — Turkish city-wall

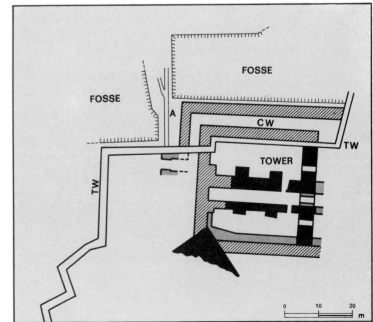

Excavation area looking east, with aqueduct in foreground

West of this stretch of the Crusader wall, the Turkish city-wall appears to have been built over the Crusader line. Built into the Crusader city-wall we found a Crusader capital in secondary use. Vincent found a similar capital in the Turkish wall, where it overlies the Crusader masonry. Close to bedrock, we also found Israelite sherds (7th century B.C.E.), as well as pottery from the first centuries C.E., mainly from the 2nd-3rd centuries. Wherever we investigated the Turkish or Crusader wall, it appeared as if it reached bedrock, and that it was

Crusader capital embedded within foundations of late Crusader wall

built into a deep foundation trench hewn into the rock.

The excavations indicate that the Crusader city-wall and tower were destroyed long before the Turkish period — possibly already in 1219, when the fortifications of Jerusalem were demolished by el-Mu'atem, the Sultan of Damascus. The stones of the tower were scattered both over the remains of the Crusader wall — which seems to have been lower than the tower — and within the fosse, to as far down as we have excavated. The Turks levelled the remains of the tower and built their wall, the present one, over it.

The north-western corner of the walls of Jerusalem has long been regarded as a key point concerning the topography of Jerusalem in the days of the Second Temple and, specifically, the course of the "Third Wall". Of the two principal theories, one identifies the line of the Third Wall with that of the present-day northern Turkish wall; the other suggestion traces it from the vicinity of the Jaffa Gate along the stretch of the Turkish wall to the north-western corner of the Old City (Zahal Square), and continues it straight towards the Russian Compound, from whence it eventually turned east to where Sukenik and Mayer discovered sections of it in 1926, (see above, pp. 60 ff.).

Several maps of the city, from 1878 on, show a section of the wall as if it continued the western course of the Turkish Wall on a straight line northward. Our excavations, however, revealed that in the section marked in the maps there are no traces of any such wall, and even if there had been some earlier wall there, the Crusader fosse would have obliterated all traces of it. In our opinion, the wall appearing on the maps is a misinterpretation of a narrow strip of 6 metres left by the Crusader quarrymen of the fosse, forming a sort of bridge separating its two parts; this provided support for an aqueduct bringing rainwater gathered on the ridge to the north of the city, leading it through a channel in the city-wall into the city.

The discovery of the fosse here, and its relatively recent date, may very well shed light on the history of the northern fosse of the city in general. The dating of this latter fosse, clearly observable in the region of the Damascus Gate and the Rockefeller Museum, is still a contested matter in scholarly circles.

The Lintels of the Holy Sepulchre

J. Prawer

Two splendid lintels formed the base of the tympana of the double portals of the Church of the Holy Sepulchre. Both lintels are carved from thin marble plaques, and are the products of Crusader artisans of the second half of the 12th century C.E. They are preserved today in the Rockefeller Museum. Together with the Crusader capitals from Nazareth, they comprise the most important examples of Crusader sculpture found in this country. The lintels were carved by two different artisans, who selected motifs far apart from one another; even the techniques employed are entirely different.

The left-hand lintel (i.e., the western one) depicts episodes from the life of Jesus prior to his crucifixion; the intention seems to have been to show events in his life which took place outside Jerusalem proper. The relief itself consists of five scenes, the central of them (unfortunately damaged) larger than the side ones. The scenes are within a squared frame, the lower edge being fitted to the tops of the capitals on either side. Interior scenes are depicted within vaulted structures, with domes and towers above. Other scenes are flanked by columns, denoting the city; these columns also serve as scene dividers.

For some unknown reason the order of the first two scenes on the left has been reversed, the story properly beginning with the second scene, at Bethany near Jerusalem. Jesus stands in the centre on a rounded stone, possibly symbolizing the universe. He is dressed with a toga over a tunic; his right hand is raised in blessing, rendered in a rather awkward manner; his left hand holds the edge of the toga, with an open book resting upon the arm in a very strange manner. His blessing is directed towards two women, Martha who kisses his feet, and Miriam who raises her hands in worship, beseeching the

Part of lintel of eastern portal

Left side of lintel of western portal

resurrection of Lazarus. The women wear veils, wrapped around and draped. Miriam is the most realistically depicted figure in this scene. Behind the two women is a group of men, elders of the city emerging from a gate. These figures are bearded, with oriental turbans on their heads; all lean on walking-sticks, and one wears a belt. To the right are four figures, the Apostles.

The second scene is the resurrection of Lazarus, within his house: At the right, Jesus holds an open book in his left hand and blesses with his right hand. Martha raises her two hands in thanksgiving. On the left, two figures roll away the stone door from Lazarus' tomb. Lazarus, revived, stands at the entrance to the tomb. He is surrounded by neighbours, witnesses to the miracle, some of whom express their surprise by raising their hands; others hold their hands to their noses, whether because of the odour of the dead or in order to hold back their tears.

The two subsequent scenes, one depicting the preparation of the Pascal Lamb and the other Jesus' entry into Jerusalem, are rather damaged. Only the right edge of the latter scene is entirely clear, with the gate of Jerusalem, palm-trees and a large crowd around. This scene is parallel to the tale related in the New Testament concerning the entrance of Jesus into Jerusalem and the crowds who shouted "Hosanna" for joy.

The final scene on the right is the "Last Supper". Framed within three arches, a curved table divides the scene horizontally; the table has carelessly been reduced to a mere table-cloth stretched over the knees of the banqueters. Beneath the central arch we see Jesus flanked by his disciples. In keeping with the depictions of this event in Medieval art, Judas Iscariot is before the table. The disciple whose head is being hugged by Jesus is traditionally John.

It is difficult to classify this relief as fine art, with its standardized composition and monotone design of the figures. Only here and there do we feel somewhat vital figures. In workmanship and technique, too, it falls behind contemporaneous Europe. The lintel in general can be said to stem from the Late Classical tradition, and similar examples are found in southern France, Provence and Languedoc.

Of an entirely different nature is the relief appearing on the other lintel. The subject, workmanship and spirit here have no relationship whatsoever with the former. This relief depicts human and animal figures within an arabesque of trees, branches, fruit and flowers. The figures are intertwined within the floral network, and the flora itself is spiralled, with a movement from left to right. The main line

Right side of lintel of western portal

of the relief is denoted by a thick branch which runs from the left in a wavy motion, forming five main medallion-like areas. Each of these is defined by a beaded branch with leaves, forming three concentric circles terminating in a sort of bud at the centre. Along the outer edge of the beaded branch are three figures, forming a triangle circumscribed by the spiral. The figures at the sides are of naked youths holding on to the branch, as if turning it. In the central medallion, however, the upper figure on the right is a centaur with bow; the figure below is a Siren with bird's body and woman's head. Between the three main medallions are similar ones, but ornamented with birds; four pairs of smaller spirals, vertically arranged and in a similar style are situated between the main medallions.

The surprising point here is the free treatment of the figures, an atypical feature for Romanesque art. The bodies are well modelled, movements are quite natural, and the harmony between the figures, their stance and the spiralling tendrils, flowers and birds is prevailing, all within a uniform geometric composition. This is in imitation of a Classical model, and the sculptor's skill is obvious.

At first glance, these reliefs recall Late Roman art. This, however, cannot have been the direct source of inspiration; the classical elements evident here were developed over the years in Europe, and also continued in the Coptic art of Egypt. Taking these two sources of influence into account, we can assume that the Crusader sculptor derived his motifs from Southern or Central Europe.

A Local Trend in Crusader Art in Jerusalem

N. Keenan

The architecture of Jerusalem in the 12th century C.E. can be regarded as an immediate product of the first Crusader kingdom (1099–1187). The refurbished Church of the Holy Sepulchre and the Church of St. Anne are regarded as having been built on contemporaneous Western patterns. On the basis of stylistic comparisons, scholars have even attempted to associate this architecture and its ornamental sculpture mainly with Romanesque art in Southern France.

Detailed examination of the remains, however, reveals evidence pointing to quite a different interpretation. Even if the plans of these structures are Western in general lines, their architectural sculpture contains a corpus of motifs drawn systematically from the vocabulary of forms specific to our region. Moreover, this sculpture could have been produced

Holy Sepulchre, capitals on left side of western portal

only by local Christian artisans, who continued local traditions held over even in times of Muslim rule. The corpus of local motifs, which is distinguished by its schematization of decorative elements and in its sparse use of figurative elements, was already crystallized in the 4th century C.E.

Was there truly a continuity of the local artistic tradition from the 6th century C.E. on through till the Crusader conquest? Can a similarity be distinguished between the forms typical to the local tradition and the forms appearing in the monumental buildings of the Crusaders?

There is no doubt that after the Muslim conquest there remained in this country a reasonably large Christian school of builders. Though no Christian buildings of the Early Arab period have survived, there exist literary sources which give details on the construction of churches and on the employment of Christian artisans in the building of monumental Muslim structures, such as the Dome of the Rock, the Great Mosque in Damascus and the palace at Khirbet Mefjer. The typical local motifs — such as the grape-tendril and the rosette-frieze — appear repeatedly in the above Muslim structures. In fact, the decorative character of the local art must have gained momentum under Muslim "non-figurative" religious restrictions.

After the destruction of the Christian churches by the Caliph el-Hakim in 1009, intensive rebuilding activity in the churches began, with Byzantine imperial patronage. In this period, el-Aqsa mosque was also refurbished, apparently by local Christian artisans. In the Crusader Jerusalem of the 12th century, the Christian communities engaged in widespread building projects. Not only did they restore their traditional buildings, they even built new ones. Though the literary sources do not mention local artisans taking part in the erection of Crusader buildings, stylistic comparison strengthens the assumption that the Crusaders did indeed employ them.

Looking at the double portal of the southern façade of the Church of the Holy Sepulchre (see above, pp. 111 ff.), we cannot but help be reminded of the Golden Gate in the Eastern Wall of the Temple Mount, built in the Byzantine period. This latter structure, a double portal, symbolized in Christian thought the triumphal entry of Jesus into Jerusalem at the beginning of the Holy Week. It may well have served as the model for the Crusader double portal of the Holy Sepulchre, symbolizing the Crusader entry into Jerusalem, yet retaining the transcendental meaning of the heavenly city.

The capitals flanking the double portal and the upper windows in the Holy Sepulchre are of a type common in this country and in Syria from the 5th century till the 11th century C.E., whereas in the West such capitals are very rare. The rosette-frieze ornamenting the arches of the double portal on the exterior is similar to that on the Golden Gate and those in churches of the 5th–6th centuries in Syria. The acanthus medallion between the two portals, a device emphasizing the symmetry of the façade, appears already on capitals of the 6th century in the Church of St. Sophia at Constantinople and on lintels and arches in the churches noted in Syria.

East of the portal there is a small chapel, used as an outside entrance to Calvary. Its windows are ornamented with two broad friezes; the western of

Detail of ornament, Golden Gate

them, above the stairs, depicts birds — such as an eagle and a peacock — among grape-tendrils. In the southern frieze small birds are seated on fruit-baskets decorated with leaves. Here too, the local artisans used motifs common in this country. The tympanum located in the inner wall of this chapel is decorated, again, with the motif of the vine with grapes.

In all the above instances, the technique of carving is typified by deep drilling, enabling a play of light and shade. In the West, this technique was extremely rare in this period.

It appears to us that only local artisans, familiar with the local corpus of motifs and with the traditional work-methods, could have repeatedly and with such regularity employed local motifs in the service of the Crusaders.

Holy Sepulchre, detail of rosette-frieze of western portal

Holy Sepulchre, frieze of western window of Calvary chapel

115

The Remains of an Ancient Synagogue on Mount Zion

J. W. Hirschberg

Though the Jews of Jerusalem were not able, after the destruction of the Temple in 70 C.E., to secure a permanent place of worship on the Temple Mount, they did establish synagogues in other parts of the city. The Bordeaux Pilgrim, who visited the Holy Land in 333 C.E., notes of Mount Zion: "Of the seven synagogues which once stood there, only one remains; the others are ploughed under and gone to seed, as Isaiah [1 : 8] has said." Similar mention of one of seven former synagogues here was made by the Church Father Epiphanius, who lived in Jeru-

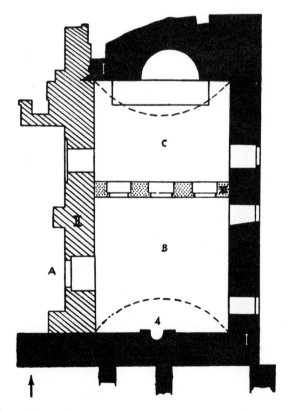

Plan of "David's Tomb". I — Roman-Byzantine walls; II — Mamluk wall; III — Turkish partition; A — outer hall; B — vestibule; C — "tomb" chamber; D — miḥrab in southern wall

salem in the second half of the fourth century C.E.

Archaeological confirmation of the existence of such a synagogue on Mount Zion was found during repairs in "David's Tomb", after the 1948 War of Independence. The late J. Pinkerfield described how, after plaster had been removed from a niche in the northern wall of the "tomb" chamber, it was found to face directly towards the Temple Mount and measured 2.48 m wide, 1.20 m deep and 2.44 m high. The finely executed masonry was typical of the Late Roman period. Further examination revealed that, within the building complex as it presently stands, the niche belongs to the initial building phase, during which the outer northern, southern and eastern walls of the chamber were erected. The original western wall is missing, the present one on this side dating from Mamluk times. A partition presently dividing the "tomb" chamber is from Ottoman times. A *miḥrab* (Moslem prayer niche) in the southern wall is dated 1452 C.E. These findings correspond with literary data on the many changes of ownership of this building.

Pinkerfield reached the conclusion that the "tomb" chamber represents a synagogue erected in the first centuries after the destruction of the Second Temple. He based this on the following factors: The construction is Roman; the niche faces the Temple site, like the niches found in the synagogues at Eshtemoa and Nave (used as Holy Arks for keeping Torah scrolls); and there is a great similarity in dimensions of the niches and in other architectural details between this building and the above synagogues. We may add that a similar niche faces Jerusalem in a synagogue at Arbel in Galilee, as well.

The antiquity of other parts of the building of "David's Tomb" was noted over a century ago by E. Pierotti, the then Municipal Engineer. His position enabled him, in 1859, to inspect those parts of the building generally closed to Christians and Jews. He noted among other things that "beneath the clay tiles in the court of the tomb, I discovered, by means of an examination I made from the exterior, the walls of an ancient Jewish building, mixed, in the parts above the floor, with later construction, which had been inserted during repairs. This can be found especially on the eastern and northern sides." Commenting on Pinkerfield's report, M. Avi-Yonah has noted plainly that these are the remains of an ancient synagogue, probably from the days of Julian (361–363 C.E.). Since the synagogue is mentioned in a source some thirty years prior to the reign of Julian, Avi-Yonah's reference would seem to be to a repair of an existing structure.

Folk tradition connects this synagogue on Mount Zion with David's Tomb. In the fourth century C.E., the Bordeaux Pilgrim thought the wall of Mount Zion to be David's Palace, and it is natural that a synagogue named in his honour should be located nearby. This would appear to be the explanation behind the Moslem tradition according to which the Caliph Omar ibn el-Khattab, upon his entry into Jerusalem, requested first to be shown to the "Miḥrab of David", that is, the niche in the prayer-room of David. In the light of the findings in "David's Tomb", there is little doubt that this refers to the niche in the "tomb" chamber there. This tradition is found in Arabic literature already in the tenth century C.E., and shortly after mention is also made of the tradition of the Jews concerning "David's Tomb" on Mount Zion.

During the Crusades, Christian traditions became attached to Mount Zion, including one which placed David's Tomb beneath the hall of Jesus' Last Supper.

In the fourteenth century C.E., the Jews and Moslems did not know the exact location of David's Tomb. An anonymous disciple of Nahmanides (probably around 1306–1312) wrote that "above the Siloam spring on the mount there is the fortress of Zion and there are the Tombs of the Kings and there is an old building which they call the Hall of David, oriented towards the Temple. There they light candles for the sanctity of the site. It is said that this is the building of David, the place where there had been the Ark of the Lord when David brought it to his house till the Temple was built." David's Hall is none other than the chamber containing the niche in its northern wall, facing the Temple Mount. It is mentioned again about 200 years later by Mujir ed-Din, the Arab historian of Jerusalem. Nahmanides' disciple mentions nothing of a tomb here, but only the site where the Ark had stood.

In the fourteenth century, the Franciscans purchased lands on Mount Zion, and the Pope placed the Hall of the Last Supper in their custody. From then on, they were in conflict with the Moslems over control of the chamber of "David's Tomb". A climax came when the Moslems triumphed and built a miḥrab in the southern wall (1452); by this time, "David's Tomb" was already "fact". Thus, the "tomb" became concrete sometime between 1350 and 1450, or thereabouts.

The niche facing the north was covered by precious carpets around 1551, and later its existence was forgotten. From the mid-sixteenth century on, Jews and Christians were forbidden entry to "David's Tomb", and only a few were privileged to descend into the "cave" and see the "tomb". Among these latter was Sir Moses Montefiore, though it is doubtful which "tomb" was shown to him. Only on Shavuot (Pentecost), the traditional date of the death of David, were Jews allowed to view the "tomb", a block in the upper storey (above the "tomb" in the chamber in question), near the Hall of the Last Supper (where the Christians, in turn, were permitted to visit only on special occasions). This situation prevailed until 1948.

Reconstruction of the Jewish Quarter in the Old City

E. Netzer

Reconstruction of the Jewish Quarter of the Old City of Jerusalem is at present in full swing. Some one hundred Jewish families and about four hundred yeshiva students are already living in the quarter, and the number of families will shortly double.

The primary aim of reconstructing the Jewish Quarter is to restore its character as a normal residential quarter, to contain some 700 families — that is, 2500–3000 inhabitants. Synagogues and yeshivas will also continue to be an integral part of the quarter, as will small shops. Upon the completion of the revitalized quarter, there will be about 150–200 shops. Of course, tourism will form the economic basis for most of these shops, and for the two or three hotels which are to rise there.

The preliminary surveys and master-plan for the quarter were prepared in 1967–1970 by a planning-team headed by the present author, on behalf of the "Company for the Reconstruction and Development of the Jewish Quarter in the Old City of Jerusalem, Ltd.", a Government company directly subject to the Prime Minister and the Cabinet "Committee for Jerusalem Affairs".

Archaeological excavations are being carried out in the Jewish Quarter wherever new structures are about to be built. In the last few years, many questions have risen concerning this scientific work — whether all planning and building should be stopped until the entire area has been investigated, or whether the entire quarter should be preserved as an open antiquities site. The present planning policy for the quarter tends in another direction, but reconstruction work has provided opportunities — possibly never to recur — for extensive excavations in this part of the city; in any event, much effort and persistence is still needed to complete the excavation of the areas available for scientific investigation.

Principles of planning and preservation. The policy adopted also strives to preserve the existing skeleton of the quarter, that is, the basic street-network and those parts of the quarter which were not badly damaged. This furthers the integration of new construction within the overall framework of the Old City and ensures a proper adherence to the city's character.

The borders fixed for the reconstructed quarter closely resemble the maximum extent of Jewish settlement here, towards the end of the 19th century. On the south, the quarter borders the city-wall; on the west — the Armenian Quarter; on the north — David and Chain Streets; and on the east — the Western Wall Plaza. The older sections of the quarter are a maze of structures from various periods, from Crusader times on. Many buildings rose with the rapid increase of Jewish population in the second half of the 19th century, mainly in the southern part of the quarter. The outstanding of these latter are the "Batei Mahse" and the adjacent "Deutsche Platz".

The quality of the buildings and of the existing street-network and their preservation were among the foremost subjects dealt with during planning. It became evident that there was a clear grid of

Air view of Jewish Quarter. (1) Batei Mahse; arched building is Bet Rothschild; (2) Block 32, restoration; (3) Block 31, centred around four Sephardi synagogues; (4) line of axis to Western Wall Plaza and bazaar; (5) arched house, with ancient "Kathros" house in centre; (6) Block 267, on left; new structures around Israelite wall, on right; (7) Block 34; (8) Block 37; (9) Block 33, with "Hurva" synagogue at centre; (10) central strip between Jews' Street and Habad Street; (11) "Terminal" area; (12) "Ari Quarter"; (13) location for "Porat-Yosef" yeshiva; (14) location for "Yeshivat Hakotel"; (15) stairs descending to Western Wall Plaza; (16) Block 38; (17) Western Wall Plaza; (18) archaeological excavations; (19) el-Aqṣa mosque; (20) Dung Gate; (21) Zion Gate; (22) Armenian Quarter; (23) Citadel; (24) Jaffa Gate.

Air view of southern part of Jewish Quarter, with Batei Mahse
in centre and Nebenzahl House at bottom

variation in the new structures — a desirable feature here. Thus, we find a "simple" approach, preserving the existing blocks but avoiding traditional elements such as the vault, dome or arch. This approach finds extreme expression in a house in the square of Batei Mahse, with its notable sparcity of windows, a feature typical of building in the Old City. The planning-team of the "Reconstruction and Development Company" tends toward this approach.

A different approach can be seen in the Nebenzahl House, designed by a team of English architects. It is noteworthy in its search for a new relationship between wall and window. Another architectural approach attempts to give more expression to modern technology in buildings, such as in the use of the dome as an element but in new materials. In contrast to all these, there is also a romantic approach, bordering on the ornamental; a clear example of this extreme approach can be seen in the apartment house east of the Armenian monastery.

Recent developments in the various activities in the Jewish Quarter can be summed up as follows:

The Batei Mahse block is nearing completion, with a paved plaza at its centre. To the west is "Bet Rothschild", one of the most impressive structures in the quarter, built in the mid-19th century and preserved almost intact. To the south is a long building, rising high above the adjacent city-wall. To the northeast and southeast, new buildings have risen.

East of Batei Mahse is the Nebenzahl House, mentioned above.

North of Batei Mahse, till Hayyei Olam Street, work in block 32 incudes mainly the restoration of existing buildings, and only in its eastern part are new structures being erected.

West of Batei Mahse, till Jews' Street, block 31 contains the four Sephardi synagogues at its centre (see below, pp. 122 ff.). We may note here especially the restoration of Gal'ed Street on the east, and of the group of houses on the west, near Jews' Street. These houses are a good example of the reconstruction and refurbishing of partly demolished structures.

In the centre of the Jewish Quarter, along the newly-cut axis street leading to the Western Wall Plaza, a ruinous area is being prepared for a future bazaar. Adjacent is the recently completed "Arches

streets, adequately serving the quarter and connecting it with the other quarters of the city. The major modification introduced was a new axis descending from the quarter to the Western Wall Plaza, now essential in the light of the huge volume of visitors to the Plaza and to the quarter; it begins in the vicinity of the Karaite synagogue and ruined "Tiferet Israel" synagogue, crosses Misgav Ladakh Street and descends on a broad stairway, the lower part of which hugs the rock-cliff bordering the quarter on the east.

The standard of architecture in most of the existing structures was rather low, though there is traditional construction of considerable quality — with vaults and arches, and free "play" between the masses and the courtyards, giving the quarter both its specific plastic scape and its particular human tone.

Detailed planning of the various buildings and blocks is being carried out by a number of architects, some of whom have had experience in similar work in the past. Planning by different architects leads to

120

House" — an apartment house in the cellar of which the ancient "House of the Kathros Family", discovered during the archaeological excavations of Prof. N. Avigad (see above, pp. 43 ff.), will be open to the public.

To the west, till the "Hurva" synagogue and the section of city-wall from First Temple times (also discovered by Prof. Avigad; see above, pp. 41 ff.), widespread building activities are taking place. (It was here that the fiercest fighting took place in 1948, and thus the area is particularly ruinous.) One lot will include shops and apartment houses, in continuation of the bazaar.

From this point till Chain Street on the north and Misgav Ladakh Street on the east, there are the best-preserved blocks in the quarter, as far as traditional construction is concerned (34 and 37). The most outstanding characteristic in Gemilut Hasadim and Misgav Ladakh Streets here is the building of parts of houses over the street proper, forming tunnels at ground level. These are one of the most impressive features of the entire Old City. In this block, reconstruction and refurbishing are the principal tasks being carried out.

In the initial stages of planning, block 33 with the ruined "Hurva" synagogue at its centre was intended as the site of a monumental synagogue (planned by an American Jewish architect), to have been the outstanding feature of the entire quarter. Execution of this plan has been delayed and is somewhat doubtful. The entire block will probably be replanned, as demanded by its central location. The Ramban synagogue, restored under the direction of architect D. Tanai, is also located in this block (see below, p. 122).

The central strip between Jews' Street and Habad Street, utilized as an integral part of the main street-network of the Old City, was the subject of a competition among architects. The winning team has begun the detailed planning; their concept involves reviving the *cardo* of the Roman city (which ran adjacent to Jews' Street) as a commercial axis, giving it the atmosphere of a bazaar.

On the south, the central strip borders an area which is to become the "terminal" of the Jewish Quarter. A street branching off from the new road between Dung Gate and Mount Zion, outside the walls, will penetrate into the Old City by means of a tunnel ending at an underground parking-facility. This latter will be hidden entirely from view but will still enable a modern way of life within the renewed quarter. Above this facility there will be apartment houses, shops, a school and a hotel. At its edge, near the "Kabrit" tower on the city-wall, an open-air theatre will be built. (In the opinion of Prof. M. Avi-Yonah, this was the very site of the theatre built by Herod the Great: if any remains of the ancient structure are found here, they will be integrated within the modern framework.)

West of Habad Street, up to the Armenian Quarter, in the section known as the "Ari Quarter", much construction work is in progress. Around the ancient "Or-Hayim" synagogue and the courtyard called "Bet Weingarten", many buildings have been refurbished, one of which is to contain the Folklore Museum of the Jewish Quarter. On the north, work is being completed on a large apartment house, and on the south, too, new structures are being built. In this area, many other buildings are being reconstructed and restored.

The area east of the Jewish Quarter between Misgav Ladakh Street and the Western Wall Plaza is of special importance because of its relationship to the plaza and the Temple Mount. Planning of the southern part is complete, and two yeshivas — the largest in the quarter — are already under construction (one is rising on the site of its premises prior to its destruction in 1948, and may turn out to be one of the most architecturally controversial buildings in the quarter).

North of the block of yeshivas, block 39 is planned to rise above the Western Wall Plaza and will form the main façade of the Jewish Quarter on the east, mostly rising above the natural rock-cliff there. Its southern part will include old buildings, typical of traditional construction in the Old City (the northern part includes partly ruined or architecturally poor structures).

Restoration of the Jewish Quarter has not yet been completed, and many more years will pass before all the dust and noise of construction settle. Even so, the day is quite near when the quarter will again take its place as a living, functioning part of the Old City and, indeed, of all Jerusalem.

Four Sephardi Synagogues in the Old City

D. Cassuto

Lacking a specific architectural tradition of their own, the Jews sought a path between Christian architectural concepts — which tend to emphasize the cruciform with a dome or other means for achieving height at the focal point — and the Moslem architectural concepts, less directional and less mystical. From the second century till the seventh century C.E., the Jews used the basilica form, but in early medieval times an archetypal form — directional but lacking all mysticism — was achieved, suitable for prayer, study and meeting alike.

The early "Ramban" Synagogue — so called even though there is no proven connection between the sage and the building — includes a hall divided down the middle by a row of columns into two aisles; this is a decided contrast to the basilical plan, with its central nave and flanking aisles. Our structure, the oldest of the synagogues known in the Old City, appears to have been converted into a synagogue towards the end of the 14th century C.E., it being suitable for public prayer and because it specifically did not resemble a church. Crusader evidence indicates that at the time it was the only synagogue in Jerusalem, shared by both Ashkenazim and Sephardim. It served as a model for other synagogues later built in the city and it is sometimes held that those in European lands imitated it as well,

Over the years, many Jews have come to regard the Dome of the Rock as the image of the Jewish Temple of antiquity, as can be seen in many naive illustrations from medieval and later times; this fact, together with the suitability of such a building-form for study and meeting, led to its being used as a model for another synagogue plan, one used for religious schools and other public buildings as well, in both Jerusalem and Europe.

Such architectural concepts among the Jews, together with their limited means, gave birth to the architectural approach seen in the four Sephardi synagogues treated here.

In 1586, the "Ramban" Synagogue was closed by order of the Turkish governor of Jerusalem, and the local Jewish community was left without a place of prayer. Subsequently, the reduced community appears to have used private dwellings for prayer, and only in the early 17th century was the first Sephardi synagogue built.

Though when the "Ramban" Synagogue was

Pre-1948 view of Jewish Quarter, looking west; on right, Nisan Beq synagogue; on left, Yeshivat Porat-Yosef

still in use, Sephardim prayed together with Ashkenazim, in a somewhat mixed rite, the new synagogue was used solely by the Sephardim. The Ashkenazi community prayed on a site adjacent to the "Ramban" Synagogue — today the court of the "Hurvah" Synagogue, while the new Sephardi synagogue was built south of the older building. Since the Sephardim represented a majority of the Jewish community in this country at the time, this new synagogue — named in honour of Yohanan ben Zakkai — became the focal-point of Jewish Jerusalem.

By 1625, the Ben Zakkai Synagogue was noted as having an additional structure adjacent to it, used for study and as a meeting hall. A European visitor noted that there were only two synagogues in all Jerusalem at this time — a small Ashkenazi building and a larger, Sephardi one with an adjoining house of study where the community council met. Thus, till the early 18th century there were only two synagogues in spite of the fact that the Jewish community had expanded considerably; this led to the study-hall of the Ben Zakkai Synagogue also being used as a synagogue, named in honour of "Elijah the Prophet".

In 1702, still only the two Sephardi and one Ashkenazi synagogues existed. But by 1842 there were two additional synagogues, mentioned in sources and already quite old at that time. A Jewish visitor to Jerusalem noted, in 1837, that one of the additional synagogues had been converted from a courtyard of the Ben Zakkai Synagogue — that is, the "Middle" Synagogue, as it is called today; and some twenty years after, the "Stambouli" Synagogue was built adjacent. He also related that the buildings were repaired in 1835, after having long been in a state of delapidation.

Thus, these four Sephardi synagogues in Jerusalem were built as follows: The Ben Zakkai — around 1606–1610; the "Elijah" — 1615–1625; the "Middle" — 1702–1720; and the "Stambouli" — around 1740.

The seating arrangement was as in all Sephardi synagogues: The bima was raised considerably above the level of the worshipers, at the centre of the hall, and Arks of the Law (double in the Ben Zakkai Synagogue) were in the eastern wall. In the "Elijah" Synagogue, the Ark is inconspicuously located near the entrance, no doubt because of the original use of the building; that in the "Stambouli"

Interior of "Elijah" Synagogue, prior to restoration

synagogue follows the pattern of the latter, the Ark being located eccentrically alongside the entrance on the east. The women's gallery in these synagogues always appears as an afterthought — formed by enclosing odd corners here or there. In general, the form of the "Middle" Synagogue was clearly influenced by that of "Ben Zakkai" and, in turn, the "Stambouli" synagogue clearly reflects the plan of the "Elijah" Synagogue.

Restoration of these buildings (see below, the following article) has regained for them their former splendour and, indeed, recently the Chief Sephardi Rabbi in Israel was once again installed in the traditional manner in the Ben Zakkai Synagogue.

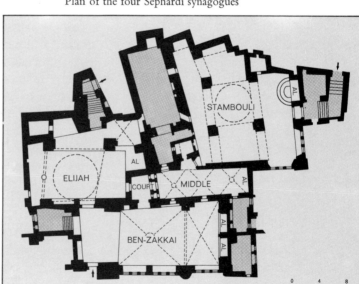

Plan of the four Sephardi synagogues

The Ben-Zakkai Synagogues—Reconstruction and Restoration

D. Tanai

The synagogue complex named after R. Yohanan ben Zakkai, belonging to the Sephardi community, is located in the heart of the Jewish Quarter of the Old City. The four synagogues, though they have common walls, greatly differ from one another. The four synagogues are known as the "Elijah the Prophet", "R. Yohanan ben Zakkai", "Stambouli" and "Middle". This is the most pleasing architectural complex in the Jewish Quarter — indeed, one of the nicest of its type in the entire country.

After the Six-Day War (1967), we found the four synagogues in ruins. Though the walls, columns, arches, vaults and domes still stood, there were many breaches. All the woodwork was missing and there was no trace of the flooring. All the interior surfaces were damp, for the stone facing on the roof had been removed, and the plaster was mouldy. Nothing, of course, remained of any of the religious appurtenances and installations or the rich interior furnishings. Between 1948 and 1967, the floor-level became raised by some three metres of debris.

When the present author was appointed as architect to restore these structures, within the framework of the activities of the National Parks Authority, several problems were evident: What was to be restored, how to restore it and where lies the thin line between reconstruction and restoration? Indeed, the aim prescribed was to restore the buildings to their former splendour, but still enable renewed use of the synagogues under modern conditions.

Our first step was to remove the debris down to the original floor-level and to scrape off the rotten plaster from the interior. At the same time, we began gathering all literary sources relevant to the synagogues, as well as drawings, photographs and the like. In spite of their prolonged existence — some four hundred years — little written evidence on the synagogues has survived, and even less pictorial data; the earliest material of value is little more than a century old.

After the buildings had been cleared and cleaned, we were able to arrive at a preliminary conclusion: These structures differ entirely from most religious buildings for, despite their considerable area (some 800 sq. m), from outside they seem hidden, with no façade; indeed, they are sunken below the street-level. The adjacent houses close in upon them and leave but narrow approaches to their entrances, from which stairs descend to the prayer-halls. No architect designed this form! Like Topsy, it just grew, within the labyrinth of houses of the Jewish Quarter.

As the preliminary work progressed, we arrived at a second conclusion: In these synagogues, there is no connection between their structural concept and architectural concepts which are governed by functional factors or any artistic and esthetic approach — individual or collective. This is most important, for it enabled us, to some degree, to distinguish between reconstruction and restoration, and to blend the two successfully.

At first, we had to examine the buildings structurally. The "Elijah" and "Stambouli" buildings were constructed according to the traditional pattern of the Byzantine-Early Arab period: "a circle on a square" — that is, a square structure with four piers supporting vaults and, ultimately, a round drum on which stands a dome. The "Ben Zakkai" and "Middle" Synagogues, in contrast, are long halls with cross-vaulting in the Moslem, Crusader-Gothic tradition. But where Byzantine, Moslem and Crusader-Gothic buildings carefully preserve symmetry, both in construction and in architecture, the synagogues here are only remotely symmetrical as far as their architectural form is concerned. Over the years, various parts of these buildings were destroyed and rebuilt (not necessarily in their original form). Often the simplest way was taken, not the preferable, in these reconstructions, as can be seen in the door and window openings, which are generally improvised. In the "Elijah" and "Stambouli" buildings, the Holy Ark was not positioned in the middle of the eastern wall, but was pushed into the north-eastern corner. There are many more deviations from the symmetry dominant in the period in which these structures were built. But whether this was intentional or incidental, a certain undefinable completeness was achieved, a perfection which cannot be ascribed to any particular architectural school — and thus the uniqueness of our complex.

In the light of the fact that there is no relationship between the structural and the architectural aspects, the reconstruction and restoration could be separated into two clear phases. In the first phase, we repaired and reconstructed the structures themselves. The thick walls were all built of stones in secondary use, no care being taken in preserving even courses. Between the stone facings of the walls was the usual gravel fill, bonded with local earth and lime. On the interior, this type of construction was clearly intended to be plastered over. Restoration proceeded according to the following principles: Exterior walls were not touched, leaving the multihued patina of ages intact; only here and there were we forced to repair or replace the masonry. To prevent penetration of rainwater through the joints, we repointed them, using suitable materials. On the interior, however, our approach was entirely different. We decided not to replaster as far as possible but, rather, to clean the stone thoroughly. Only several of the walls, of very rough masonry, had to be replastered. Most of the piers, arches, ribs and mouldings were left unplastered, while the domes and vaults — all of rough masonry — were resurfaced with new plaster. This system of emphasizing the old stone surfaces and exposing piers and arches — even though they had previously been covered — enabled us to ascertain the many modifications which had taken place over the centuries, interesting changes which plaster could only hide.

From the few remains of the original flooring and roof-paving, we ascertained that slabs of colourful Jerusalem stone were used throughout. Thus, we resurfaced all the roofs with this material; unfortunately, we could not obtain sufficient slabs of

Holy Ark in Ben-Zakkai synagogue; above, pre-1948; middle, as in 1967; bottom, during restoration work

the right colour for the interior floors, and a lighter shade of Jerusalem stone was used. Only in the "Ben Zakkai" Synagogue was the floor restored with its original network pattern in black; the white Italian marble of the background, however, was replaced by a light marble-like stone.

Only after all these structural repairs, which were intended to preserve all the ancient features of the buildings, could we proceed to the architectural aspects.

From the few drawings and photographs available, we became familiarized with the interior as it was in the last century; this was supplemented by some first-hand knowledge of the buildings as they were prior to 1948. This material aided us considerably in our design. Thus, prior to 1948, there were small windows in the drums of the domes, resembling normal wooden windows. Since these are 12 m above floor-level, it is clear that they were never opened or cleaned; thus, we preferred to use here stone frames with disc-panes, resembling such windows throughout Spanish-Moslem architecture.

The *bimah* of the "Ben Zakkai" Synagogue had been of the traditional form with six steps, the "seventh step" being used for the reading of the Torah. Around the *bimah*, 60–100 worshippers could sit on benches lining the walls. We were requested to provide for several hundred worshippers, and the tall, imposing *bimah* of the past, with all its beauty, did not suit this prerequisite. A different *bimah* had to be designed, one which would not hide the Holy Ark behind. Thus, we conceived of a *bimah* in the style of those in the Sephardi synagogues in Safed and Jerusalem, though we provided only one step. This *bimah* allows for 250 worshippers without crowding, each of whom can see the entire synagogue interior without hindrance.

We also concluded that antique furniture suited the synagogues much more than modern, and thus we were pleasantly surprised and grateful when the late Dr. U. Nachon obtained two Holy Arks from Italy, some 400–500 years old, for the "Elijah" and "Stambouli" Synagogues. Only in the "Ben-Zakkai" Synagogue did we restore the original Ark; this was built of stone in Gothic style. The inner surfaces were tiled, as in the Sephardi synagogues in Istanbul. The doors were made by the artist Bezalel Schatz; these doors, and the three entrance doors, were especially designed by artists, keeping in mind their full significance. The main door to the "Stambouli" Synagogue was designed by Buki Schwarz; that of the "Ben Zakkai" Synagogue by Bezalel Schatz; in the "Elijah" Synagogue, the door is by Shraga Weil.

We were careful to ensure that each of these works possessed a definite, Jewish character. Thus, Buki Schwarz's design encompasses the *menorah* as its main motif; Bezalel Schatz utilized Hebrew letters as his central theme on his door; and the mural above the Ark in the "Ben Zakkai" Synagogue, by Jean David, expresses the concepts of Earthly Jerusalem and Heavenly Jerusalem.

Many more details could be elaborated upon; in any event, all our efforts were focussed upon one end — preserving as much of this precious heritage as possible, taking into account its more-than-historical nature.

The National Park in Jerusalem

D. Dvir

Since the Six Day War, with the renewal of activity in urban planning in Jerusalem, a national park has become a central element in the city's image. Immediately after the war, certain areas and landscapes were in danger of being swallowed up — city features with a history of 2000 years, destroyed in an instant. Tens of thousands of visitors and pilgrims flood the city, without sufficient paths, parking-places and other facilities having been prepared for them. And building in the city is outpacing the planners.

The proposal to form a national park around the walls of the Old City, which was presented to the Prime Minister several weeks after the 1967 war, aimed to preserve the historical open space around the city; to form a green-belt setting off and ensuring the uniqueness of the Old City; and to develop the area to absorb the crowds of visitors in a manageable manner.

In order to harmonize planning, a master-plan was prepared for the National Park. It is intended — and is indeed serving — to integrate the separate, specific plans within an overall framework. This plan is based on the principle that the city-walls and the surrounding valleys should retain their character which, if possible, should be emphasized by clearing and planting.

The belt of valleys formed by the Hinnom and the Kidron surrounds the Old City on the west, south and east. In the valley-beds are gardens, with olive and fig trees, palms and vines. On the slopes of the valleys there is a broken belt of greenery. The trees are pine and cypress, predominantly dark green in colour. Along the city-walls is a further strip of greenery — grass, wild flowers, shrubery — all quite low and allowing for a full view of the walls.

The first phase of the plan — some 2000 dunams around the Old City — has already been approved and put into motion. A subsequent phase involving some 1,500 additional dunams, including the Mount of Olives and Mount Scopus, already appears in the Jerusalem Master Plan as intended for a National Park.

The broad lines of the plan for the park have found approval among planning bodies in Israel and abroad, and the various religious and international bodies in Jerusalem are cooperating fully in this project. On the west and south, the Government has been able to purchase considerable land for this purpose, thus preventing its future misuse. The detailed planning has been completed for the western flank, for the Mount of Olives and for Mount Scopus.

In the early stages of planning, one faction wished to set the Old City apart from the New, whereas another group wished to integrate it by continuous building in the gap between; there were those who sought to bring broad approach-roads up to the very city-walls, wheras others sought to keep all private traffic far away from the Old City. It was soon obvious that the key to any successful plan lay in the matter of the road-system around the Old City.

Any modern road-network immediately adjacent to the old walls would clearly dwarf them and rob them of all proportion. It was thus decided to remove the major arteries from the western area of the park, at least optically. To preserve the green landscape and the existing topography, and yet to allow clear pedestrian access, parts of the main roads will run through tunnels. A pedestrian tunnel will run beneath the walls to provide direct access into the Old City.

Subterranean parking-lots are planned in two centres — near Jaffa Gate and near Damascus Gate; these underground structures will also provide various tourist facilities. The considerable financial outlay in this respect will undoubtedly delay execution of this aspect of the plan for some time.

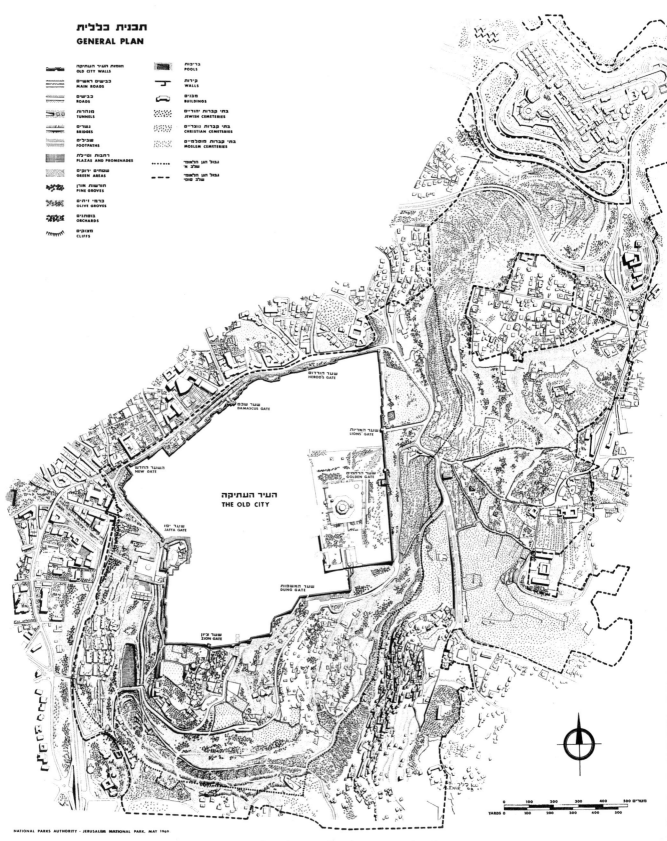

Plan of National Park to surround Old City

So far, the route to the Western Wall has been cleared by the formation of an outer ring-road and a road along the western ridge, as a sort of "panorama drive". An attempt is being made to separate pedestrian and motor traffic as far as possible.

Another factor aiding in the realization of the concept behind the park is the crystallization of a clear and forceful policy concerning building. Doubts were expressed in the early stages of planning concerning the huge proportions which construction in Jerusalem is taking on, proportions far outstripping even the most optimistic estimates. The walls of the Old City — the height of which generally does not exceed ten metres — seem mighty when isolated, but in the shadow of some even modest sky-scraper, they would seem puny. Thus, we have formulated a tripartite principle: The proportions of a building are to be determined by the proximity to the city-walls; construction adjacent to the walls and in the valleys is to be avoided; and massive multi-storeyed structures are to be far removed from the Old City. The latter part of this principle is still the subject of a somewhat heated controversy. Other principles include the redesigning of the eastern façade of New Jerusalem in the Mamilla district, reconstruction of historical quarters such as Yemin Moshe, the clearance of ruins as in Shama‘ and the upper Hinnom valley. Another as yet unsolved problem concerns the preservation of the picturesque character of Silwan village, for there is no sense in trying to make life there stand still.

A widespread network of pedestrian paths, of some 20 kilometres total length, is planned to meet the special needs of the various types of visitors. For the crowds of tourists, and to preserve the close daily contact between the Old and New Cities, a promenade is being built to surround the Old City walls on the north, west and south. This is not a simple sidewalk, but a broad promenade separated from the bustle of traffic and surrounded by greenery. These areas are becoming "parks" in themselves, places for rest and enjoyment of the cityscape. So far, the central portion of the promenade, from Jaffa Gate to near Damascus Gate, has been completed. The network of paths will also serve to connect the various sites of interest within the National Park.

Mitchell Park opposite Citadel

National Park along city-wall, leading to Jaffa Gate

A large Herodian house on the western hill (Jewish Quarter Excavations, 1974), with the Temple Mount in the background

TABLES OF MAJOR ARCHAEOLOGICAL ACTIVITIES IN JERUSALEM SINCE 1863

Y. SHILOH

The tables and maps are intended to present briefly the archaeological-historical investigations in Jerusalem in the last 112 years. Only the major activities could be included, outlining the results concerning the various remains and monuments. The data are provided in a generally chronological order by region, with the excavators' conclusions as to dating and identification (occasionally modified in the light of more recent research).

LEGEND OF PERIODS

EB = Early Bronze Age (32nd–23rd cent. B.C.E.)
MB = Middle Bronze Age (22nd–16th cent. B.C.E.)
LB = Late Bronze Age (16th–13th cent. B.C.E.)
1T = First Temple period (10th–6th cent. B.C.E.)
2T = Second Temple period (6th cent. B.C.E. – 70 C.E.)
Hel. = Hellenistic period (Late 4th cent. – 37 B.C.E.)
Her. = Herodian period (37 B.C.E. – 70 C.E.)
Rom. = Roman period (70–324 C.E.)
Byz. = Byzantine period (324–638 C.E.)
(Dates approximate)

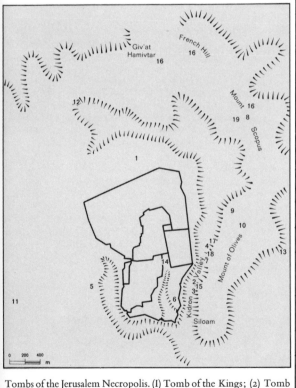

Tombs of the Jerusalem Necropolis. (1) Tomb of the Kings; (2) Tomb of Pharaoh's Daughter; (3) Royal Steward's Tomb; (4) Absalom's Tomb; (5) Herod's Family Tomb; (6) Tomb of Davidic Dynasty; (7) Zachariah's Tomb; (8) Nicanor's Tomb; (9) Dominus Flevit; (10) Mount of Olives, western slope; (11) Jason's Tomb; (12) Sanhedria Tombs; (13) Mount of Olives, south-eastern slope; (14) Western hill, eastern slope; (15) Silwan village; (16) Northern ridge group; (17) Jehoshaphat's Tomb; (18) Bene Hezir Tomb; (19) Nazirite Tomb.

	Tombs	Water Installations
F. de Saulcy 1863, 1865	1863, partial clearance of *Tomb of the Kings*, 1st cent. C.E.; 1865, *Tomb of Pharaoh's Daughter* in Silwan, 1T.	
Ch. W. Warren 1867–70		Discovered *Warren's Shaft*, LB(?); examination of *Gihon Spring*, Bronze Age on; *Siloam Tunnel* and *Pool*, 8th cent. B.C.E. on; *Strouthion Pool* (with Clermont-Ganneau, 1870); *Birket Israil* (both latter, 2T).
Ch. Clermont-Ganneau 1869–1871	1869, *Tomb of the Kings*, Her.; 1870, examined *Royal Steward's Tomb*, Silwan village, 1T; 1871, cleared façade of *Absalom's Tomb*, Her.	
White Friars and K. Mauss 1871		Cleared *Bethesda* (Probatica) *Pool*, 2T till Byz.
H. Guthe 1881		Thorough investigation of *Siloam Tunnel* and *Pool*, 1T.
C. Schick 1886–1901	1891, cleared *Herod's Family Tomb*.	1886, 1901, cleared *Gihon Spring*; examined external channels southward, 2T on; 1880, published *Siloam Tunnel Inscription*, 8th cent. B.C.E.
M. Parker (and L. H. Vincent) 1909–11		Cleared *Warren's Shaft*, LB(?); investigated water supply in *Gihon Spring* and *Siloam Tunnel*.
R. Weill 1913–14, 1923–24	Excavated *Tomb of Davidic Dynasty* in southern part of City of David, 1T (area used as quarry, Her.)	
N. Slouschz 1924	Final clearance of *Absalom's Tomb*; partially cleared *Zachariah's Tomb*.	
E. L. Sukenik 1925–46	1928–29, cleared *Nicanor's Tomb* on Mt. Scopus, Her.; 1926–46, cleared 38 tombs in around city, 2T.	
N. Avigad 1945–47, 1967; 1968–	Tomb monuments in *Kidron brook*: *Tomb of Pharaoh's Daughter*, *Tomb of Royal Steward*, 1T; *Absalom's Tomb*, *Cave of Jehoshaphath*, *Tomb of Bene Hezir*, *Zachariah's Tomb*, Hel.–Her.; 1967, *Mt. Scopus*: *Tomb of Nazirite Family*, 1st cent. C.E. (see above, pp. 66–67).	*Jewish Quarter*: cisterns, baths, drainage channels, Her.
P. Bagatti and G. Milik 1953–55	*Dominus Flevit* — western slope of *Mount of Olives*: clearance of rich cemetery, Hel.–Byz., mainly Her.	
P. Saller and P. Lamer 1954	Western slope of *Mount of Olives*: cleared cemeteries, MB–LB.	
L. Y. Rahmani 1954	*Jason's Tomb*, Rehavia, Hel.; tombs in *Sanhedria* area, 2T.	
H. Statchbury 1960	Final clearance of *Zachariah's Tomb*.	
K. M. Kenyon 1961–67	South-eastern slope of *Mount of Olives*: shaft-tombs, MB I.	*Area F*: examination of walls damming lower Tyropoeon valley (nothing earlier than Hel. — mostly Her. and Byz. — of dams and pools).
B. Mazar 1968–	Tombs on lower eastern slope of *Western Hill*, 8th–7th cent. B.C.E. (see above, pp. 38–40).	South-western corner of *Temple Mount*: aqueduct and cisterns, Her.; cisterns, 1T (see above, pp. 25–40).
D. Ussishkin 1968	Survey of tomb-caves in *Silwan village*, 1T (see above, pp. 63–65).	
Various 1968–	Tomb-caves with ossuaries: *Mount Scopus, French Hill* and other sites (see above, pp. 67–74).	
A. Mazar 1969		Survey of aqueducts from *Hebron–Bethlehem* region, 2T and later (see above, pp. 79–84).
J. Margovski 1970–71		Turkish aqueduct near *Burj Kabrit*.
D. Bahat and M. Ben-Ari 1971–72		*Zahal Square*: Crusader aqueduct (see above, pp. 109–110).

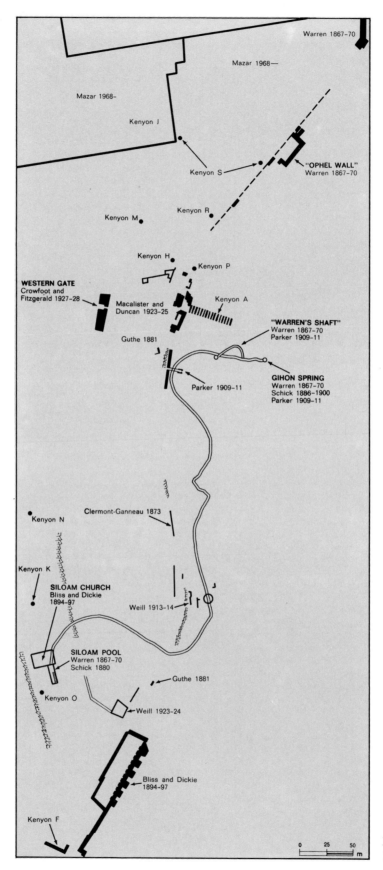

Warren 1867–70

Mazar 1968—

Mazar 1968–

Kenyon J

Kenyon S

"OPHEL WALL"
Warren 1867–70

Kenyon M

Kenyon R

Kenyon H

Kenyon P

WESTERN GATE
Crowfoot and
Fitzgerald 1927–28

Macalister and
Duncan 1923–25

Kenyon A

"WARREN'S SHAFT"
Warren 1867–70
Parker 1909–11

Guthe 1881

Parker 1909–11

GIHON SPRING
Warren 1867–70
Schick 1886–1900
Parker 1909–11

Kenyon N

Clermont-Ganneau 1873

Kenyon K

SILOAM CHURCH
Bliss and Dickie
1894–97

Weill 1913–14

SILOAM POOL
Warren 1867–70
Schick 1880

Guthe 1881

Kenyon O

Weill 1923–24

Bliss and Dickie
1894–97

Kenyon F

0   25   50
m

Excavations in the City of
David (see Table)

	Old City and Vicinity	Temple Mount; City of David, North and West	City of David, East	Jewish Quarter and Mount Zion
Ch. Wilson 1867–68	Examination of façade of *Holy Sepulchre*, Crusader.	Discovery of *Wilson's Arch*, Her.		
Ch. W. Warren 1867–70	Trial excavations in *Muristan*; *Qal'at Jalud* (city-wall and tower fragment), late 2T (?); *David Street* (city-wall fragments and two towers of *First Wall*).	Trial shafts to bedrock around walls of *Temple Mount*, Her. on; base of pier of *Robinson's Arch*, Her; examination of *Wilson's Arch* and structures to west (with Ch. Wilson); examination of *Solomon's Stables*, Her. (?) on.	*Ophel Wall* and tower, probably no earlier than Her., reused in Byz. (Eudocia's wall, 5th cent. C.E. ?).	
H. Modsley 1871–75				Remains on line of *First Wall* at southwest corner of *Upper City* (Bishop Gobat's School); traces of quarrying and fosse.
Ch. Clermont-Ganneau 1873–74		Examination of *Antonia* region (Her.) and *Ecce Homo Arch* (Rom.); discovery of *Temple Inscription* forbidding entry of Gentiles.	*City-wall* fragment (20 m long), 2T.	
White Friars and K. Mauss 1863–76, 1888–1900	Discovery of church remains overlying *Probatica Pool*, St. Anne's (1879), Byz.			
H. Guthe 1881			*City-wall* fragments and dwellings, 2T.	
C. Schick 1886–1901		1891: Report on clearance of *Golden Gate* by Ottoman authorities.		
F. J. Bliss and A. C. Dickie 1894–97		*Siloam Church* over Siloam Pool, mid-5th cent. C.E.	*City-wall* fragments at SE corner of *Eastern Hill*, at end of Tyropoeon valley, 1T to Byz.	*City-wall* fragments and towers on S slope of *Mt. Zion*, 2T and Byz.; city-wall fragments, quarrying and fosse forming line to NE above *Tyropoeon valley* (apparently inner wall protecting E flank of Upper City), Hel.–Her. (?); dwellings and street fragments, Byz.
M. Parker (and L. H. Vincent) 1909–11			Building and fortification fragments, on E slope.	
L. H. Vincent 1910–13	Examination of city-wall fragments (*Third Wall*) at *Qal'at Jalud* (1912); Mt. of Olives: 1910, *Eleona Church*; 1913, *Church of Ascension*, Byz.			
P. G. Orfali 1909, 1919–20	*Gethsemane Church*, Byz.			
R. Weill 1913–14, 1923–24			*City-wall* fragments (20 m long); southern gate (?); square guard-tower; all 1T. Round tower, Hel.; discovery of *Theodotos Inscription*, 1st cent. B.C.E.	
R.A.S. Macalister and J. G. Duncan 1923–25		*City-wall* fragments in N, ascribed to Jebusite and earliest Israelite cities; apparently no earlier than Rom.–Byz.	*Jebusite wall*, two towers and glacis, held to be of Jebusite and earliest Israelite cities. Kenyon (see below) ascribes them to early 2T, mainly Hel. *Ophel Ostracon* discovered.	
E.L. Sukenik (with L. A. Mayer) 1925–27, 1940	Excavation of parts of wall and towers on line of *Third Wall* on N of city, between "Italian Hospital" and northern extremity of Kidron brook, mid-1st cent. C.E.			
J. Germer-Durand 1889–				Byz. church on premises of *Church of St. Pierre in Gallicantu*; dwellings and stepped street in same area, 2T and Byz.
J. W. Crowfoot and G. M. Fitzgerald 1927–28		*City-wall* and *western gate*, ascribed to Israelite through Hel. Kenyon (see below) ascribes them to no earlier than Hel.		
R. W. Hamilton 1931, 1937–38	1937–38, excavation of foundations of *Damascus Gate*: Her. remains; gate of *Second Wall*; gate of Rom. and later periods. Trench E of *Herod's Gate*, foundations of N face of Old City Wall — fragments of city-wall of Aelia Capitolina, Rom.			1931, *Tyropoeon valley*, paved street, drainage channels, Her. on.

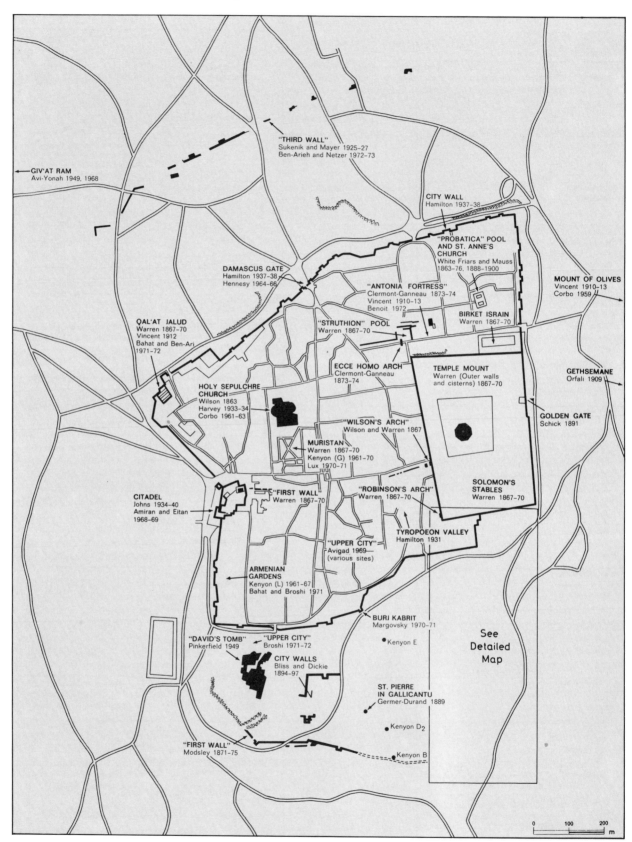

GIV'AT RAM
Avi-Yonah 1949, 1968

"THIRD WALL"
Sukenik and Mayer 1925–27
Ben-Arieh and Netzer 1972–73

CITY WALL
Hamilton 1937–38

"PROBATICA" POOL
AND ST. ANNE'S
CHURCH
White Friars and Mauss
1863–76, 1888–1900

DAMASCUS GATE
Hamilton 1937–38
Hennesy 1964–66

"ANTONIA FORTRESS"
Clermont-Ganneau 1873–74
Vincent 1910–13
Benoit 1972

MOUNT OF OLIVES
Vincent 1910–13
Corbo 1959

QAL'AT JALUD
Warren 1867–70
Vincent 1912
Bahat and Ben-Ari
1971–72

"STRUTHION" POOL
Warren 1867–70

BIRKET ISRAIN
Warren 1867–70

ECCE HOMO ARCH
Clermont-Ganneau
1873–74

TEMPLE MOUNT
Warren (Outer walls
and cisterns) 1867–70

GETHSEMANE
Orfali 1909

HOLY SEPULCHRE
CHURCH
Wilson 1863
Harvey 1933–34
Corbo 1961–63

"WILSON'S ARCH"
Wilson and Warren 1867

GOLDEN GATE
Schick 1891

MURISTAN
Warren 1867–70
Kenyon (G) 1961–70
Lux 1970–71

CITADEL
Johns 1934–40
Amiran and Eitan
1968–69

"FIRST WALL"
Warren 1867–70

"ROBINSON'S ARCH"
Warren 1867–70

SOLOMON'S
STABLES
Warren 1867–70

"UPPER CITY"
Avigad 1969
(various sites)

TYROPOEON VALLEY
Hamilton 1931

ARMENIAN
GARDENS
Kenyon (L) 1961–67
Bahat and Broshi 1971

BURJ KABRIT
Margovsky 1970–71

• Kenyon E

See
Detailed
Map

"DAVID'S TOMB"
Pinkerfield 1949

"UPPER CITY"
Broshi 1971–72

CITY WALLS
Bliss and Dickie
1894–97

ST. PIERRE
IN GALLICANTU
Germer-Durand 1889

• Kenyon D₂

"FIRST WALL"
Modsley 1871–75

• Kenyon B

0   100   200
m

Excavations in Jerusalem (see Table)

134

	Old City and Vicinity	Temple Mount; City of David, North and West	City of David, East	Jewish Quarter and Mount Zion
W. Harvey 1933–34	Examinations of *Church of Holy Sepulchre*, remains from Byz. on.			
C. N. Johns 1934–40	Excavations in *Citadel*: wall and towers, Hel.; Herodian repairs and construction of *Phasael Tower* ("David's Tower"); remains of camp of Roman Tenth Legion overlying Herod's Palace; part of W city-wall of Aelia Capitolina, Rom.			
J. Pinkerfeld 1949				Trial-excavation of foundations in *David's Tomb*, Mt. Zion; apse discovered, possibly of synagogue Rom. (see pp. 116–117).
M. Avi-Yonah 1947, 1968	*Giv'at Ram*, W Jerusalem: remains of camp of Roman Tenth Legion; church and monastery, Byz.			
V. Corbo 1959, 1961–63	1959, summit of *Mt. of Olives*: *Church of Ascension*, Byz. 1961–63, examinations in *Church of Holy Sepulchre*.			
K. M. Kenyon 1961–67	*Area C (Muristan)*: 2T, in excavator's opinion, outside line of "Second Wall"(?), traces of fosse of which were found; in Rom., area filled and levelled, being included within Aelia Capitolina; dwellings, Byz.	*Area G (Ḥakuret el-Khatuniyye,* S of SW corner of Temple Mount): remains of splendid public building, Early Arab (but ascribed to Rom.–Byz. by excavators; with R. de Vaux). *Areas K, M, N*: Israelite construction at top of hill; Hel. dwellings, cut by city-wall of late 2T; paved area of street; Her.; overlying remains of destruction of 70 C.E., Byz. settlement. Further evidence of gap in settlement of area of "City of David" in Rom. and early Byz., till 5th cent. C.E. (Excavator suggests N line of defences of "City of David", through areas A-P-H-M).	*Area S*: Thick wall of ashlar masonry, 8th cent. B.C.E. — S line of wall on S of Temple Mount (?). *Area A*: pottery from EB on; remains of city fortifications at lower end of sectional trench, from 18th cent. B.C.E. till end of 2T; supporting terrace walls of city on slope ("Millo" ?), from LB till destruction of 1T; remains of dwellings of above periods, on abovenoted terraces; above, fortifications of 5th cent. B.C.E. on, mainly Hel. (the "Jebusite wall"). *Areas A, H, R*: Clear evidence of absolute destruction of city in 70 C.E.; above, Byz. dwellings.	*Areas B, D₁, D₂, E* (on slope of *Mt. Zion*): In excavator's opinion, no remains earlier than period of Agrippa I found; thus, earliest settlement on Mt. Zion and its fortifications no earlier than mid-1st cent. C.E.; traces of dense settlement, especially in Byz. *Area L* (in *Armenian Quarter*): Pottery of 8th–6th cents. B.C.E.; remains of walls, Persian period (?); objects from camp of Roman Tenth Legion; dwellings, Byz.; remains of Mamluk market.
J. Hennessy 1964–66	Revealing of early gate beneath *Damascus Gate* (ascribed to *Third Wall*, with repair and use in Rom.–Byz.).			
B. Mazar 1968–		S and SW of *Temple Mount*: remains from Her. on (see above, pp. 25–40).		
R. Amiran and A. Eitan 1968–69	Excavations in *Citadel*: Iron II, Hel. Her. Rom.–Byz. remains (see above, pp. 52–54).			
N. Avigad 1969–				*Jewish Quarter*, various sites: Israelite settlement, 8th cent. B.C.E. on; Hel., Her., Byz., Arab remains (see above, pp. 41–51).
U. Lux 1970–71	Investigations beneath *Erlöser Kirche*; segment of wall and fill, 1st cent. C.E.			
J. Margovsky 1970–71				Excavation adjacent to *Burj Kabrit*: Base of tower, prior to 12th cent. C.E.; Byz. street segment; part of paved street, Her.
D. Bahat and M. Broshi 1971				Excavations in *Armenian Garden*: Her. and Crusader remains (see above, pp. 55–56).
M. Broshi 1971–	Excavations adjacent to SW segment of Turkish city-wall; segment of *First Wall*, Hel. on.			Excavations on *Mt. Zion (Armenian churchyard)*: Iron II, Her., Rom., Byz., early Arab, Crusader remains (see above, pp. 57–59).
P. Benoit 1972	Investigation of *Lithostrotos*, 2T, Rom. (see above, pp. 87–89).			
D. Bahat and M. Ben-Ari 1971–72	*Zahal Square*: Crusader remains (see above, pp. 109–110).			
S. Ben-Arieh and E. Netzer 1972–73	Excavation near American Consulate on N of city: Remains ascribed to *Third Wall* (late 2T); remains of monastery (?), Byz.			

Tunnel beneath "Single" Gate (Excavations near the Temple Mount, 1974)

BIBLIOGRAPHY

Amiran, Ruth. "The First and Second Walls of Jerusalem Reconsidered in the Light of the New Wall." *IEJ* 21 (1971): 166–67.

———, and Eitan, A. "Excavations in the Courtyard of the Citadel, Jerusalem, 1968–1969. Preliminary Report." *IEJ* 20 (1970): 9–17.

———. "Herod's Palace." *IEJ* 22 (1972): 51–52.

Avigad, N. "Excavations in the Jewish Quarter of the Old City, Jerusalem. Preliminary Reports." 1969–70, *IEJ* 20 (1970): 1–8; 1970, 20 (1970): 129–40; 1971, 22 (1972): 193–200.

———. "The Burial-Vault of a Nazirite Family on Mount Scopus." *IEJ* 21 (1971): 185–200.

Avi-Yonah, Michael. "The Newly Found Wall of Jerusalem and Its Topographical Significance." *IEJ* 21 (1971): 168–69.

———. "The Third and Second Walls of Jerusalem." *IEJ* 18 (1968): 98–125.

Ben-Arieh, Sara, and Netzer, E. "Excavations Along the 'Third Wall' of Jerusalem, 1972–74." *IEJ* 24 (1974): 97–107.

Ben-Dov, B. M. "The Omayyad Structures near the Temple Mount." In *Excavations in the Old City of Jerusalem near the Temple Mount. Preliminary Report of the Second and Third Seasons, 1969–1970*, edited by Benjamin Mazar. Jerusalem, 1971.

———. "Building Techniques in the Omayyad Palace near the Temple Mount, Jerusalem." *Eretz-Israel* 11 (1973): 75–91 (Hebrew).

Ben-Eliezer, S. *Destruction and Renewal. The Synagogues of the Jewish Quarter*. Jerusalem, 1973.

Broshi, M. "The Expansion of Jerusalem in the Reigns of Hezekiah and Manasseh." *IEJ* 24 (1974): 21–26.

Cresswell, K.A.C. *Early Muslim Architecture* I/1. Oxford, 1932. I/2. Oxford, 1969.

———. *A Short Account of Early Muslim Architecture*. Harmondsworth, 1958.

Encyclopaedia of Archaeological Excavations in the Holy Land II, edited by M. Avi-Yonah. Jerusalem, 1976: 579–641.

Grafman, R. "Nehemiah's 'Broad Wall.'" *IEJ* 24 (1974): 50–51.

Haas, N. "Anthropological Observations on the Skeletal Remains from Giv'at ha-Mivtar." *IEJ* 20 (1970): 38–59.

Hamilton, R.W. *The Structural History of the Aqsa Mosque*. Oxford, 1949.

Hecker, M. In *Sefer Yerushalayim*, edited by M. Avi-Yonah. Jerusalem, 1958: 213–28, and esp. the bibliography on p. 427 (Hebrew).

Israel Exploration Journal. 22 (1972): 171–72.

———. 24 (1974): 285.

Kenaan, Nurith. "Local Christian Art in Twelfth Century Jerusalem." *IEJ* 23 (1973): 167–75; 211–29.

Kenyon, Kathleen M. *Digging Up Jerusalem*. London, 1974.

———. *Jerusalem*. London, 1967.

Mazar, Benjamin. *The Excavations in the Old City of Jerusalem. Preliminary Report of the First Season, 1968*. Jerusalem, 1969.

———. *The Excavations in the Old City of Jerusalem near the Temple Mount. Preliminary Report of the Second and Third Seasons, 1969–1970*. Jerusalem, 1971.

Naveh, J. "An Aramaic Tomb Inscription Written in Paleo-Hebrew Script." *IEJ* 23 (1973): 82–91.

———. "The Ossuary Inscriptions from Giv'at ha-Mivtar." *IEJ* 20 (1970): 33–37.

Pinkerfield, J. *Battei Ha-Kenisiyyot Be-Erez Yisrael (Synagogues in Palestine)*. Jerusalem. 1946.

Rosenthal, E.S. "The Giv'at ha-Mivtar Inscription." *IEJ* 23 (1973): 72–81.

Sharon, M. "Arabic Inscriptions from the Excavations at the Western Wall." *IEJ* 23 (1973): 214–20.

Simons, J. *Jerusalem in the Old Testament*. Leiden, 1952.

Tzaferis, V. "Tombs at and near Giv'at ha-Mivtar, Jerusalem." *IEJ* 20 (1970): 18–32.

Ussishkin, D. "The Necropolis from the Time of the Kingdom of Judah at Silwan, Jerusalem." *Biblical Archaeologist* 33 (1970): 34–46.

Vincent, H. *Jerusalem sous terre*. London, 1911.

INDEX

ERRATA

Page 14, left, 4th line from bottom:
    For temonos *read* temenos

Page 23, caption:
    Add to (6): Off map at top left

Page 43, right, 8th line from bottom:
    For p. 44 *read* p. 42

Page 55, right, note, 2nd line:
    For 400–1000 *read* 400 × 1000

Page 55, in caption:
    For Southern wing of Crusader palace *read*
    Crusader palace and city-wall

Page 83, 4th line from bottom
    For (19) *read* (29)

Page 104, right, 8th line from top:
    For p. 115 *read* p. 105

Page 112, left, 6th line from bottom:
    For Pascal *read* Paschal

Page 116, in plan:
    For 4 *read* D

DATE DUE

MR 7 '85			
GAYLORD			PRINTED IN U S.A